MANAGEMENT BY OBJECTIVES
A SELF-INSTRUCTIONAL APPROACH

WILLIAM C. GIEGOLD
Virginia Polytechnic Institute and State University

MBO

LEADER'S MANUAL
TO THE MBO SERIES

McGRAW-HILL BOOK COMPANY
New York / St. Louis / San Francisco / Auckland / Bogotá / Düsseldorf
Johannesburg / London / Madrid / Mexico / Montreal / New Delhi
Panama / Paris / São Paulo / Singapore / Sydney / Tokyo / Toronto

**LEADER'S MANUAL
TO THE MBO SERIES**

MANAGEMENT BY OBJECTIVES
A Self-Instructional Approach

Copyright © 1978 by McGraw-Hill, Inc.

ISBN 0-07-023189-3

234567890 DODO 7832109

This book was set in Univers by Allen Wayne Technical Corp.
The editors were Robert G. Manley and John Hendry;
the designer was Anne Canevari Green;
the production supervisor was Jeanne Selzam.
R. R. Donnelley & Sons Company was printer and binder.

CONTENTS

PREFACE

This book was designed to help organizations begin the complex process of implementing management by objectives (MBO), using the three main volumes of this series, entitled *Management by Objectives: A Self-Instructional Approach*. It is addressed to the executive who will be assuming the leadership of the MBO implementation effort in the organization; to the person assigned to monitor and advise on the progress of implementation; to trainers who may find themselves leading a schedule of work sessions during the start-up phase; and to any manager who wishes to practice the participative approach to learning with one or more subordinates.

In fact, the material in this manual will be helpful when *any* two or more involved people feel the need to get together and exchange ideas about the MBO system, whether their need is to come to a consensus on the top-priority goals of their component, or to provide each other with feedback on their styles of conducting a performance appraisal. By using the exercises in the three self-instructional volumes and the group methods and exercises in this manual, you can build (with the help of your group) an MBO system to meet the specific needs of your organization. This group effort will also help ensure the support and mutual understanding of the managers and individuals involved, and will therefore greatly improve your chances of successful implementation.

The three volumes are self-instructional in the sense that an individual reader who has completed the exercises in them will have a thorough understanding of—and will have practiced—the principles and methods of MBO. The reader will also have experienced many of the problems and pitfalls of implementation, and will be capable of installing an MBO system in his or her own organizational component.

For broader use of MBO, however—especially when transcending departmental or functional dividing lines—you will need something more than the sum of the individual impressions and understandings your managers or professionals will have derived from their separate studies. Accordingly, the activities in this manual are designed to promote the cross-fertilization of ideas and the mutual understanding that enable group processes to produce better results than any individual could produce working alone.[1]

For the leader who has not yet read the three main volumes, a brief summary of their contents is in order. Our objectives for the whole series, as presented to the reader in each volume, are:

1. To facilitate understanding of the management system known as MBO
2. To identify and describe the elements which make up the MBO system and the interpersonal skills which enhance the chances of its successful implementation

---

[1]The three volumes also contain a number of exercises designed primarily for the use of the individual, which are not generally suited to the group discussion format. These deal with such subjects as personal time management, individual career and job strategies, self-assessment of the motivation to manage, and analysis of the feedback needs of a manager's employees. For examples, see Exercises 3, 8, and 9 in Vol. I, Exercise 3 in Vol. II, and Exercise 6A in Vol. III.

3. To give the reader an opportunity to develop the required skills and to experience some of the problems and pitfalls that may arise in implementing MBO

4. To help the reader develop a management system that adapts the general principles of MBO to the specific needs of his or her organization

VOLUME I: STRATEGIC PLANNING

This volume begins with a general overview of the MBO system. (A similar overview is included at the beginning of each of the other two volumes for the convenience of those organizations and individuals who are concerned with the topics covered in only one or two of the books.) Next, Vol. I develops the concept of *strategy* as the positioning of the resource strengths of the organization or the individual in order to achieve the greatest impact on the desired results. The remainder of the volume analyzes the strengths and weaknesses of the organization compared with the needs and wants of client groups and others who have claims on the organization—suppliers, employees, the public, etc. Similar comparisons are made with what the competition is doing, and attention drawn to the strengths needed to cope with the future demands of the rapidly changing social, political, technological, and economic environment. This inventory of needs, strengths, threats, and opportunities provides the basis for resource allocations and concentrations, enabling the selection of sound organizational objectives. Throughout the first volume, a parallel analysis on the individual level allows the reader to plan his or her personal career and job strategies.

VOLUME II: OBJECTIVE SETTING

Volume II describes how these broad organizational objectives are translated first into more detailed objectives at lower organizational levels, and then into personalized objectives for the individual manager or professional worker. A series of guidelines is provided to improve the ability of an objective to fill its three main functions: (1) to clearly document an organizational need, (2) to facilitate measurement of progress in filling that need, and (3) to motivate the worker to achieve the desired end. The sources of objectives are treated in some detail, including the individual job description and the organization's key results areas. *Results* must be achieved in all these areas in order to say confidently that the firm is turning in a good total performance. The various types of objectives are covered — routine, problem-solving, and innovative — as well as some of the major reasons for the failure of objectives to perform their three main functions. Several areas in which objectives can be very productive but are notoriously difficult to set — for example, objectives for supporting staff functions and for hourly-paid workers — are also discussed.

We then turn to the interpersonal, one-to-one relationship between manager and employee that is crucially important to the success of MBO, and discuss the strengthening of that relationship through the process of joint objective setting. Since the ability to convert objectives into performance is of such importance to the future of both the organization and the individual, we next discuss *validation* — the determination that an objective has a reasonably high probability of successful completion, given that the employee works diligently and competently toward it. Validity is best assured by sound action plans, and we complete the discussion of objectives in Vol. II with an introduction to some of the more useful tools of project planning — problem-solving models, techniques for ranking alternative solutions, and network methods for project scheduling.

VOLUME III: PERFORMANCE APPRAISAL

Volume III covers the performance appraisal process, starting with a brief history of the development of the results-based MBO appraisal system. This system concentrates on the achievement of planned objectives, but also admits personality-related evidence in the determination of an individual's overall performance.

The critical incident approach to personality problems is described. It is an approach which avoids pejoratives such as "aggressive," "uncooperative," and "abrasive," and helps the individual change by describing the problem and its solution in terms of observable behavior. This is followed by a detailed discussion of the methods and problems of measuring performance.

Next, the elements of a sound performance appraisal system are presented, including the four types of employee contacts necessary for full effectiveness of the process: (1) day-to-day informal contacts, (2) the periodic progress review, (3) the less frequent overall appraisal of performance and potential, and (4) the salary review discussion. Several subsequent chapters provide the reader with some basic principles of motivation, employee development, and interpersonal communication (supplementing those in Vol. II) to help make employee contacts more fruitful. The volume concludes with a discussion of the knotty problem of relating pay to performance.

As you take on the duties of leadership in implementing MBO, you may find that your "followers" have outdistanced you as a result of having already gone through the guided tour we have just described. If so, we recommend that you catch up as quickly as possible by familiarizing yourself with the contents of the three volumes and the exercises therein. In this manual you will find advice that will help in shaping your perspective on the applicability of MBO to your organization and in avoiding the major pitfalls of implementation. We have included detailed suggestions on how to run productive meetings designed to reach consensus on organizational issues, and how to achieve creative solutions to problems. There is also a great deal of material on the role-taking method for teaching the type of interpersonal communication that will make your joint objective-setting discussions and performance appraisal meetings truly productive.

While this manual teaches the process (*how* to conduct group sessions), the content (*what* the sessions should cover) is based on the exercises in the three main volumes. Listed in the usage table that follows are some of the more commonly encountered subject areas for group work. The table indicates the appropriate exercises from the main volumes and the sections of this manual that will be of help. We have subdivided the topics under two headings: (1) organizational issues, which address the general question of how to design and install an MBO system tailored to your needs, and (2) the skills required by everyone taking part in the system to make it most effective.

When both you and your group have read the appropriate

X

Usage Table

Meeting Topic	Individual Readings and Exercises (Volume and Unit)	Applicable Sections of Leader's Manual
Organizational Issues		
a. Assessing the need for MBO	I; II; or III–1 (Exercise A)	I; II–A, B; III–A
b. Diagnostic questions about the organization	II–4	I; II–A, B; III–A
c. Testing the group's understanding of MBO principles	I; II; or III–1 (Exercise B)	II–D
d. How well does the organization serve its .claimants?	I–4	II–A, B
e. Assessing strengths and weaknesses of the organization	I–5	II–A, B
f. Assessing and predicting environmental trends	I–6	II–A, B
g. Developing product and functional strategy	I–7, 8	II–A, B, C
h. Selecting organizational objectives	II–4, 5	II–A, B, C
i. Developing staff objectives	II–7 (Exercise B)	II–A, B, C
j. Developing and selecting alternative action plans	II–9	II–A, B, C
k. Assessing the organization's performance appraisal system	III–2, 3, 6 (Exercise 6B)	II–A, B
l. Use of forms in implementation	III–6 II – Figures 6, 7, 8, 10 III – Figures 3, 4, 5, 6, 7	III–B, C
Skill Building		
m. Writing sound objectives	II–3	II–A, B
n. Conducting the joint objective-setting session	II–8	II–D, E
o. Appraising personality factors affecting performance	III–4	II–D, E
p. Conducting progress review, performance appraisal, and salary discussions	III–7, 8, 9	II–D, E
q. Setting priorities or ranking alternative courses of action	II–9	II–A, B
r. Using the network method to plan a project or program	II–10	II–A, B, C

material and completed the exercises individually, we suggest that you start with meetings based on topics a, b, and c (assessing the need for MBO, diagnostic questions about the organization, and testing the group's understanding of the MBO process), using these meetings for the purpose of obtaining consensus. If the group is starting from scratch, start with the same topics, but *assign* the appropriate readings and exercises as individual work, allowing sufficient time for completion before you schedule the group session.

From that point, you are on your own. But be selective in your use of the material for group purposes. For example, you may not want to involve everyone in more strategic topics such as f, g, and h (assessing and predicting environmental trends, developing strategy statements, and selecting organizational objectives). (However, don't overlook the value of setting strategy at the departmental or lesser component level, or even at the level of the individual manager or professional.)

Finally, it is not our purpose to make professional trainers out of managers who may be leading their groups in an educational endeavor such as this for the first time. In some situations, the advice and assistance of a specialist in your own training or human resources development component may be required. The services of an outside consultant-facilitator can also be helpful, especially when the boss prefers to take part in the training as a participant rather than as a leader.

By and large, however, the group methods described herein are well within the capability of nonprofessionals in the training field. The experience of leading a group in the use of these methods can be exciting and rewarding to all concerned. Good Luck!

William C. Giegold

SECTION 1

ASSESSING THE NEED FOR MBO IN YOUR ORGANIZATION

SOME PLAIN TALK ABOUT MBO FOR THE LEADER*

As a leader of your company's MBO implementation effort, you will have a major influence on the acceptance of the program by the people with whom you work and on the level of enthusiasm with which they respond to the demands you will be making of them. Your own attitudes and feelings about MBO will be a major factor in the type of influence you exert. With that in mind, we cannot risk having you feel that you have been sold a bill of goods. Instead, we want you to be fully informed about what organizational results you can reasonably expect from MBO, and in what kinds of situations. This introductory section is our attempt to do the best we can to

---

*Portions of this section are adapted from "MBO After All These Years," *The Conference Board Record,* vol. 12, no. 7, pp. 48-52, July 1975. Used with permission of the publisher, The Conference Board, Inc.

1

inform you, without knowing the specifics of your organization. We hope that it will stimulate your thinking about where to look for the results, and how to structure a system that will be most productive for your organization. But above all, we want you to approach the task with realistic expectations.

The literature is by no means filled with tales of resounding success in applying MBO. Rather, one reads a mixed bag of equivocal progress reports and, increasingly, critical or skeptical reviews of the concept itself.[1]

In some cases, the criticism results from not understanding what MBO is all about. But there are other reasons underlying the failure of MBO systems to live up to their promise. We feel that one of the most important is that MBO has been sold to many an organization without regard for the specific needs, strengths, and weaknesses of the management and the employees. Frequently, the difference between failure and success lies merely in finding the true role for MBO, which may serve well in the appropriate application. We want to call your attention to the applications and conditions in which MBO is most likely to be successful.

MBO: NEW TECHNIQUE OR OLD HAT?

George Odiorne, a pioneer in articulating MBO as a system of management, defines it as a management process whereby the supervisor and the subordinate, operating with a clear definition of the organizational goals and priorities established by top management, jointly identify the individual's major areas of responsibility. These areas are defined in terms of the results expected of the individual, and used as guides for operating the unit and assessing the contributions of each of its members.

We discuss this definition at some length in the overview of each volume, but it should be clear at a glance that MBO is *not* a new technique. In fact, it is a good description of the system of management that better managers in more effective organizations have always used. It is, in effect, a definition of good management.

---

[1] See, for example, A.A. Imberman, "The Low Road to Higher Productivity," *The Conference Board Record*, vol. 12, no. 1, pp. 29-37, Jan. 1975; W.E. Rothschild, *Putting It All Together: A Guide to Strategic Thinking* (New York: AMACOM, 1976), pp. 2-4.

And since most managers tend to think of themselves as *good* managers, a frequent reaction to reading Odiorne's or anyone else's definition is "But that's what I'm already doing!"

This may or may not be true. By way of analogy, take *time* management, currently one of the most popular subjects in the field of management gimmickry. Executives are enthusiastically flocking to seminars on the subject, where they "learn" such earthshaking techniques as holding shorter meetings, giving more work to the secretary, and not reading every word on every piece of paper that crosses their desks. The editors of *Business Week* comment:

> **"** *Teaching time management is mostly common sense. But obvious as some of the lessons are, most executives can profit by putting them into practice.* **"** [2]

The concepts contained in MBO—and those of some approaches to time management (see Vol. I, Unit 3)—are a little more sophisticated, but they should be equally obvious to the thoughtful executive. Obvious or not, however, there is ample evidence that executives can benefit from MBO as well as from hot tips on time management. For example, another recent *Business Week* article quotes the current chief executive officer of a major U.S. corporation:

> **"** *We became a sales-oriented organization, assuming the more volume we had, the more money we would make. We simply did not put sufficient emphasis on profitability. We have tried far too long to be all things to all people.* **"** [3]

It is tempting to say that a well-conceived MBO system would not have allowed such a state of affairs to develop. However, the quotation makes clear the role of *assumptions* in contributing to the problem. We are the first to admit that MBO contains no magic that will prevent executives from making the wrong assumptions, or from choosing the wrong goals or objectives. What MBO *does* do is force the executive to examine goals and objectives in all key results areas

---

[2] *Business Week,* March 3, 1975, p. 68.
[3] *Business Week,* March 17, 1975, p. 50.

important to long-term survival and growth, and to think about the relationships and possible conflicts among objectives. This thought process will *help* in choosing the "right" objectives, but it is still no guarantee.

THE PROBLEM OF MEASURING MBO'S EFFECTIVE- NESS

The article quoted above[4] concludes by stating that "in trying to make an imprint on the company, the CEO has been able to perk up its performance in a favorable economic climate; now the question is whether the new style will enable it to prosper in a far less benevolent economic environment."

Herein lies a major difficulty in evaluating any new management style or technique. Like the performance ratings on mutual funds, the evaluation must rate effectiveness over one or more complete cycles. Unfortunately, the effectiveness of programs like MBO is made difficult to measure by users' lack of persistence in economic downturns and reversion to panic-type remedies, often accompanied (or caused) by a change in top management.

The track record of MBO, based strictly on achievement of the promised rewards of improved profitability or organizational effectiveness, is indeed mediocre. Even John Humble, an internationally known MBO consultant, admits that benefits are very difficult to evaluate:

> *Some of the improvements would have occurred anyway, some would have taken longer; some would not have been thought of, or would not have come to fruition.* [5]

In the case of British Colt Industries, a situation publicized extensively by Humble in both film and book form, a company official concludes:

> *At the time of writing— two years after the start of MBO— it is too early to give an overall indication of the effect on Company overheads. Net profit . . . is likely to reflect other influences than a change in managerial effectiveness.* [6]

---

[4]Ibid., p. 50.

[5]John W. Humble, *Management by Objective in Action* (London: McGraw-Hill, 1970), p. 28.

[6]Ibid., p. 45.

Another team of researchers found significant differences, after MBO was introduced, in the form of more positive employee attitudes, better knowledge of their bosses' goals, and a greater ability to communicate with their bosses. But the researchers readily admit that attempts to relate the adoption of MBO to improved organizational performance are few and far between. In fact, the one instance cited showed a *deterioration* of economic performance following an all-out introduction of MBO, a finding that the researchers, like Humble, attribute to "coincidence," or the operation of uncontrollable outside influences.[7] This may sound like a cop-out, but let's face it—chance occurrences such as an unexpected breakthrough in the research department, an economic decline, the rise or fall of a major competitor, or any number of other factors, frequently have such a tremendous impact that they mask completely the results of an organizational change such as MBO.

ATTITUDE CHANGE AND PERFORMANCE IMPROVEMENT

An improvement in employee attitude is probably the most frequently reported result from the introduction of MBO. Whether or not "gung-ho" attitudes become translated into positive results is determined by uncontrollables working for or against the organization, as well as by the work climate, which may either facilitate or hinder the translation. In spite of this, however, even the most hard-shelled antibehavioralist would not claim that positive attitudes have absolutely *no* effect on organizational performance.

For example, one manager remarked to us, after perspiring through a long weekend of work planning with his top management team in an introductory phase of MBO:

> **❝** *For the first time in a number of years, I'm going to show up for work tomorrow knowing that I've got a purpose greater than just to make it through the day!* **❞**

Only time will tell whether his level of effort and performance will increase as a result, but he apparently had something going for him that he did not have before.

---

[7]S.J. Carroll, and H. L. Tosi, Jr., *Management by Objectives: Application and Research* (New York: Macmillan, 1973), pp. 121-123.

6

WHAT MBO
IS NOT

Many reasons have been given to explain why MBO so often fails.[8] Advocates of MBO sometimes appear to be building an impenetrable barrier to ward off criticism of the system. The reasons they give for failure invariably reflect the manager's lack of commitment to it or misapplication of it.

Even though this notion may be unpalatable to the practicing manager, there are, in fact, several psychological barriers in the way of a rational decision on MBO. These can lead to disappointment or to rejection of the concept before it becomes fully functional. These barriers arise primarily from great expectations that the introduction of an MBO program will somehow provide automatic control over an organization, preventing it from going astray.

A list of some of the things that MBO is *not* may help to place it in perspective.[9]

First, MBO is not a program that can be superimposed on an ongoing system of policy and procedure, in a "set it and forget it" approach, and be expected to produce change. This approach will produce only increased impatience and frustration in subordinates overwhelmed with the added paperwork. The impatience most often results in a ritualistic routine of annually revising objectives, and then filing them away to be revised again next year. When top management adopts MBO, expecting to set it and forget it, it need look for no improvements except perhaps in isolated pockets where highly motivated individuals may use the process and discover things they never knew before about their jobs and about themselves. For example, one bank department manager, using a set of simple forms to itemize his key areas of responsibility, goal statements, and performance standards, quickly filled twenty pages describing each detailed phase of his job. When we warned that he was in danger of drowning in a sea of paper, rather than benefiting from MBO, he replied:

> " *Don't knock it! This has given me the first chance in a long while to sit down and analyze just what my job is all about.*

---

[8]See, for example, Dale D. McConkey, "20 Ways to Kill Management by Objectives," *Management Review,* October 1972, pp. 4-13; and James Owens, "The Value and Pitfalls of MBO," *Michigan Business Review,* vol. 26, no. 4, pp. 11-14, July 1974.

[9]These are also listed in the overview units of Vols. I, II, and III. Read the complete overview to get a synopsis of what your group members have covered in their individualized study.

*Now that I've got it all laid out, I can begin setting some
priorities for action.* **99**

Clearly, even the ritual aspects of MBO can lead to unexpected
benefits for the individual.

It is true that, at least in the early phases, the paperwork associated with MBO can take a lot of the manager's time. Our
admittedly hard-nosed reaction to this complaint is that "nobody
promised you a rose garden." Sound management is a full-time job,
and if you haven't been working hard at it, now is the time to get
started. Paperwork can be a problem but it is also a necessity, and
the *real* problem lies in determining the difference between what is
dross and what is paperwork with a purpose. Unfortunately, in the
initial phases, paperwork may appear to many participants to *be* the
purpose.

Second, MBO is not an easy road to improved organizational
effectiveness. There is no easy road. Those who are practicing the
management trade most successfully (and success here should be
measured over periods that include both upturns and downturns)
know that it is a full-time job and a difficult one at that — and MBO
does not and is not meant to make it any easier. Like most worth-
while skills, a good deal of effort is required to attain it, and the
rewards that an organization gains from mastering MBO are likely to
be proportional to the additional demands that it makes on the management group.

Likewise, MBO is no panacea. It will not salvage a business that
is in a dying industry; it will not eliminate your competitors nor the
need for wise decision making and priority setting. Intellectual
ability, vision, and intestinal fortitude are, and will continue to be,
qualities that separate the exceptional executive from the crowd, and
MBO will not supply these. It can, however, help to identify weaknesses and development needs in the company's management.

Finally, it is not just another behavioral science technique
involving "industrial democracy" and "self-determination" — phrases
that warn most practicing managers to steer shy. However, the
major authorities on the concept have no illusions on this score.
Odiorne states:

66 . . . *it's true that participative management is perfectly
acceptable as one method of goal-setting in the MBO sys-*

tem. As a system, however, MBO works also by autocratic or top-down goal-setting. The choice of which method to use, or when to mix them, is determined more by the demands of the situation, especially the expectation of subordinates, than by the basic nature of the system itself. In fact, the system is really neutral to such value judgments. **"** [10]

and Humble adds:

" *MBO should be thought of as a top management planning and control approach rather than an aid to the personnel function.* **"** [11]

To summarize, MBO is a tough, demanding prescription for managing, designed for intelligent, highly motivated managers — nothing more, nothing less.

WHO SHOULD CONSIDER USING MBO?

MBO works best in an organization where there is:

1. A heavy commitment to improved effectiveness on the part of higher management
2. A well-thought-out organization structure in which responsibilities and areas of authority are clearly spelled out and understood
3. An organizational climate in which interfunctional cooperation is an accepted way of life
4. An ability of managers to communicate on a continuing, informal, productive basis with their employees, and vice versa

An organization that already rates high in all these respects is one that is least likely to need MBO and least likely to see any major effects as a result of introducing it. However, because they rate high on prerequisite 1 — commitment and receptiveness to change — the managers in such an organization are likely to embrace any new concept so as not to overlook a technique that may be useful. Just as

---

[10]George S. Odiorne, *Management by Objectives* (New York: Pitman, 1965), p. 140.

[11]Humble, op.cit., p. 263.

the people who come to church are generally recognized to be those who least need the sermon, so the manager most likely to be inspired by MBO may be the one who least needs it.

Where, then, should an MBO system be prescribed? If the principles of MBO aren't a pretty good *des*cription of what you are already doing, you should consider them to be a *pres*cription. However you were taught to define management (or otherwise came to view the management game) — as a constellation of processes such as planning and organization; as essentially a job of motivating people; as the process of maintaining a set of relationships among subsystems and the environment; or simply as a means of mobilizing resources to satisfy present or future market needs — MBO can either describe or prescribe an overall approach that makes sense.

MBO cannot, in itself, make a sick organization well. Health in an organization is to a large degree a result of its purpose, direction, and climate, which combine to enhance success in favorable environments and minimize failure in hostile environments. A more useful way to look at MBO is as a diagnostic tool or a "discloser" — an agent which reveals the clarity of the organization's direction and the status of its climate, and ultimately how well or how badly management is doing its job. The true usefulness of MBO may be as a tool for the newly appointed top executive or newly reawakened management team, to help them lead an ailing organization back to full effectiveness.

MBO may hold real promise for your organization as a diagnostic tool, and as a system of planning, analysis, and control, rather than as a quick and easy behavioral science cure for all organizational ills. In Exercises 1A and 1B, we present diagnostic questions that a soundly conceived and implemented system of MBO should enable your group to answer positively. A very high ratio of affirmative or favorable answers (assuming your people have answered the questions honestly and thoughtfully) would indicate little or no urgency to embark on a program of MBO for your whole organization. On the other hand, if the number of unsatisfactory answers is high, major changes may be indicated.[12]

---

[12] Your group members, if they have completed their study of Vols. I and II, have already answered these questions for themselves. This gives you the opportunity to hold group exercises to reach consensus or gain support in addressing the major problems, or to identify organizational components for selective application of MBO.

Unless you and your colleagues perceive the need for such major changes in the overall system of top management planning and control, MBO as a companywide effort may not be the best approach. A strong incentive to change on the part of higher management (and the realization of everyone in the organization that top management is commited to that change) is necessary if you are to install a meaningful MBO system that will benefit the whole organization.

Introduction of MBO should still be considered in organizational components in which one or more of the following measures is necessary:

1. Diagnosis of a sick organization or component
2. Rapid analysis by a new manager of an unfamiliar component and its key people
3. Introduction of an atmosphere of change into a static organization
4. Rapid and forceful introduction of the philosophy of a new leader into an ongoing organization

MBO has unquestioned value as a discloser of organizational weakness in the structural, personnel, and communication areas. In helping you recognize and correct these weaknesses, MBO enables you to translate into tangible results the improved work attitudes that many organizations have reported following its introduction. Without prior analysis and corrective action, the attitude change is likely to be short-lived and generally nonproductive.

But above all, apply MBO in proportion to the need, selectively within the organization if so indicated. You may also use the various techniques covered in this series selectively to improve your performance appraisal procedures, sharpen the precision and validity of your written objectives, or improve your company's strategic planning process. Selectivity and the tempering of your expectations will help you to get the most out of MBO.

Don't set your expectation level too low, however. One of the myths that has become associated with MBO is that it takes 3 to 5 years to make MBO an effective force in an organization. It is true that time must be spent making certain that top management thoroughly understands the implications of MBO and that persistence and patience are necessary to see results. Nevertheless, many organizations have found the improvement curve to look like Fig. 1,

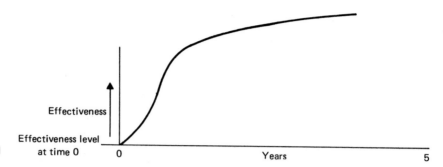

FIGURE 1

with substantial results achieved in the first 6 to 12 months. An organization that experiences an improvement curve like Fig. 2 over the first few years (1) has employed the wrong consultant, (2) is not truly committed to the effort, (3) needs a drastic overhaul of its human resources, or (4) has made a poor investment in the MBO implementation program because of an already high level of managerial competence and organization.

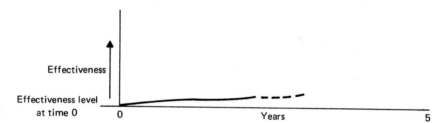

FIGURE 2

GROUP ASSESSMENT OF THE NEED FOR MBO

The two exercises that follow appear elsewhere in this series. Exercise 1A appears in Unit 1 of Vols. I, II, and III; Exercise 1B is in Vol. II, Unit 4. If your group members have already completed these exercises individually, we suggest that you use the results as the basis for a consensus-seeking meeting, as described in Sections 2A and 2B of this manual. If not, you may assign the exercises to your group as the task to be completed in the first phase of such a meeting.

Either exercise may be used profitably in two consecutive sessions: the first to *define* the organizational status and major needs for improvement, the second to *select* from these the highest priority targets for action.

In all such diagnostic exercises, the critique can easily get out of hand. Just as a flock of chickens will attack an injured bird en masse at the first sight of blood, a group of people discussing their organizational situation will quickly seize on such scapegoats as "policy" or "management" as the source of all problems, once the first mention is made of them. As the leader, you must be alert for this "bleeding chicken" effect and take prompt measures to eliminate it, because it subverts the rational decision-making process. Do not hesitate to break in on any such discussion, pointing out the group's responsibility to look on *themselves* as agents of change, whether the needed changes be in a policy area, in breaking a communication barrier with higher management, or whatever.

EXERCISE 1A

Assessing the Need for MBO

1. List the critically important duties, responsibilities, and results which your job should, under ideal conditions, contribute to the organization.

2. List any other duties which interfere with your fulfilling the critical obligations listed above.

3. List any problems (organizational, procedural, policy, interpersonal, etc.) which prevent you from contributing to the organization as effectively as you wish.

4. Referring to the MBO definition and flow process diagram shown in the overview units of Vols. I, II, and III, select the most critical interferences and problem(s) you have identified. In which aspect or element of MBO might you expect to find an answer or a solution? Describe possible action and the results expected.

EXERCISE 1B

Diagnosing Organizational Needs

Rate your organization on a scale of 0 to 10 on each of the twenty diagnostic questions below:

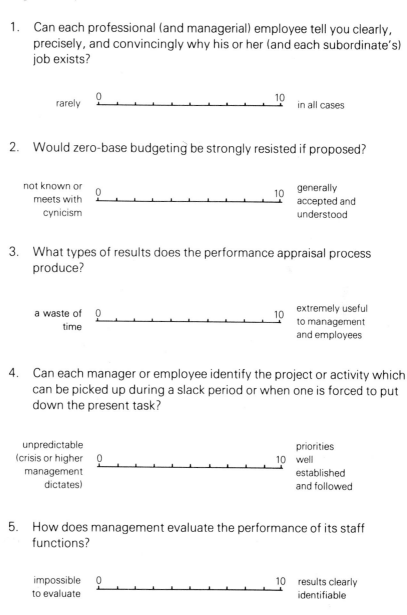

1. Can each professional (and managerial) employee tell you clearly, precisely, and convincingly why his or her (and each subordinate's) job exists?

    rarely 0 ⊢──────────────10 in all cases

2. Would zero-base budgeting be strongly resisted if proposed?

    not known or
    meets with 0 ⊢──────────────10 generally
    cynicism   accepted and
                                      understood

3. What types of results does the performance appraisal process produce?

    a waste of 0 ⊢──────────────10 extremely useful
    time   to management
                                      and employees

4. Can each manager or employee identify the project or activity which can be picked up during a slack period or when one is forced to put down the present task?

    unpredictable
    (crisis or higher 0 ⊢──────────────10 priorities
    management   well
    dictates)   established
                                             and followed

5. How does management evaluate the performance of its staff functions?

    impossible 0 ⊢──────────────10 results clearly
    to evaluate   identifiable

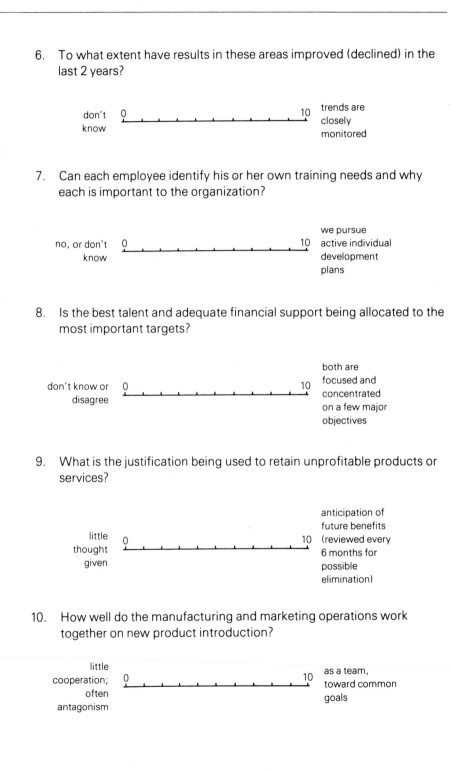

6. To what extent have results in these areas improved (declined) in the last 2 years?

don't
know 0 ——————————— 10 trends are closely monitored

7. Can each employee identify his or her own training needs and why each is important to the organization?

no, or don't
know 0 ——————————— 10 we pursue active individual development plans

8. Is the best talent and adequate financial support being allocated to the most important targets?

don't know or
disagree 0 ——————————— 10 both are focused and concentrated on a few major objectives

9. What is the justification being used to retain unprofitable products or services?

little
thought
given 0 ——————————— 10 anticipation of future benefits (reviewed every 6 months for possible elimination)

10. How well do the manufacturing and marketing operations work together on new product introduction?

little
cooperation;
often
antagonism 0 ——————————— 10 as a team, toward common goals

11. What procedure is followed to drop or cancel a project or program that ceases to show promise or contribution?

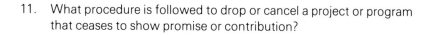

no procedure,
mainly continued
by advocacy

procedure clearly
defined and
followed

12. If funding for development or operations were cut by 10 percent, what activities or personnel would be disengaged?

little
thought
given

clearly
identified

13. Which key people in the organization can normally be counted upon to set tight standards? To overcommit? To hold back?

no basis
for judging

each manager
knows and
works with
subordinates
on this

14. Can our current level of overall performance be traced to specific areas of organizational strength (or weakness)?

little
thought
given

clearly
identified

15. Are resources being allocated to the areas of strength? Are corrective efforts or management's attention focused on areas of weakness?

little
thought
given

appropriate
plans made
and action
being taken

18

16. Are the high performers in the organization rewarded significantly differently from the average? Are the low performers?

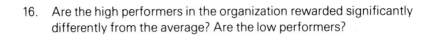

not identified, or all treated alike — 0 ——————— 10 — compensation tied to performance

17. Does each manager or professional know what his or her level of performance is?

have not discussed it; don't know — 0 ——————— 10 — yes; by both compensation and other feedback

18. How frequently do the ideas of lower and middle management and professional personnel result in changes in top management thinking?

seldom; little credit given — 0 ——————— 10 — often; ideas are sought, valued, and rewarded

19. To what degree have performance standards been tightened in the past 3 years for production or line operations? Staff operations?

no change, accept current performance — 0 ——————— 10 — tightened and achieved

20. To what extent is organizational success measured in terms of *results*, rather than *activity* per se?

few measurements used except in production areas — 0 ——————— 10 — as much as possible; looking for better ways

SECTION 2
CONDUCTING GROUP ACTIVITIES

A. A TASK-ORIENTED MEETING FORMAT

A task-oriented meeting format that produces results using small-group methods is designed to reach a common conclusion, decision, or course of action given a wide range of initial opinion. This format is suitable for group sizes from eight to thirty, since it provides a range that goes from two subgroups of four persons each to five groups of six persons each.

Selection of Subgroups

For content-oriented meetings — those involving analysis of your organization, planning, problem solving, or decision making[1] — the

---

[1] These meetings may serve other purposes — to introduce the concept of consensus, to work on interpersonal issues interfering with group performance, or to experiment with other aspects of group dynamics. We refer you to the *Handbooks of Structured Experiences* and the *Annual Handbooks for Group Facilitators,* published by University Associates, La Jolla, Calif., for the theory and practice of conducting such process-oriented group activities.

subgroups should be designated in advance by the leader, so as to include the widest possible range of knowledge, perspectives, and skills that can be brought to bear on the problem being considered.

Research has shown that the optimum size of a subgroup ranges from four to seven. Fewer than four persons limits the variety of skills and viewpoints represented and is below the "critical mass" necessary to sustain a productive discussion. With more than seven members, it is difficult to maintain the continual involvement and identification with the group of all members. It is not necessary to avoid even numbers for the sake of preventing tie votes; voting as a means of forcing a group decision is not a recommended practice. Instead, a consensus is the more desirable outcome of a group discussion. See Section 2B for an explanation of the consensus-seeking process.

Provide in advance, for each subgroup, a work table sufficiently large to allow each person to do paperwork separately from the others, but small enough to allow conversation in a normal tone of voice and to achieve physical closeness. (Six people grouped around a 6 by 2½ ft. table is about right.) Try to avoid arrangements in which three or more persons sit facing in the same direction; such arrangements make eye contact among members difficult and hinder psychological closeness. Tables should be separated enough to prevent distraction caused by cross talk from other subgroups.

Before breaking up into subgroups, provide appropriate instructions to the assembled group on the common task to be completed. The task—the same for each subgroup—is to reach a decision, a solution, or a recommendation by consensus, and to report its findings through its chosen representative to the assembled group. Each report is to be summarized on flip chart paper and posted in view of the group. The representatives, in a panel discussion, must then attempt to reach an overall consensus for the total group, reconciling whatever differences between the subgroups may have emerged. The representatives should, of course, remain open to suggestions from their own constituents, to assure that they fully convey the sense of their subgroups.

The Subgroup Discussions   If group members have already worked individually on the task at hand (for example, on Exercise 1B), the subgroup discussions can begin as soon as any questions about the task are answered. The individual solutions become the basis for the subgroup discussion. If the members are approaching the task cold, it will be necessary to allow sufficient time for individual work before proceeding. You should allocate the time available for the total meeting among the several stages as described below.[2] In the event that the subgroups finish their discussions in less than the allotted time, it is essential that you move along promptly. Noise level is the clearest indicator that a subgroup has finished its task. A silent group or a quiet room is a signal for you to inquire into the status of the discussion. You must be alert for this lull in activity, because there is a natural tendency for most groups to resume a healthy level of conversation (on topics not necessarily related to the meeting objectives) after the task is finished.

A more likely problem is that one or more of the subgroups will not be finished when your schedule requires that you move on to the next phase. This can often be corrected by making a general announcement about 15 minutes before your deadline that "representatives should now be preparing their presentations."

The Panel Discussion Reassemble the group with the representative panel up front, and give each representative the opportunity to report. Limit questions by other representatives (and the audience) to requests for clarification only. Do not allow discussion of the merits of each report at this point.

When all reports are made and posted in view of the whole group, start the representative panel discussion. This has as its objective a *single* solution or recommendation for the overall group. At the start of this phase, review the rules for consensus seeking and encourage the panel to be creative in synthesizing an overall solution that may be better than any of those proposed by the subgroups.

In view of the investment your organization has already made in this meeting, it is advisable that you, or a ranking executive, act as

---

[2] A minimum of 2 to $2\frac{1}{2}$ hours should be allowed for a meeting of this kind. A subgroup discussion period of 45 minutes and a panel discussion of 45 minutes to an hour will probably be necessary to explore thoroughly an organizational issue of any major consequence.

moderator of this discussion, especially when working with an inexperienced group. This will convey the seriousness of the organization's commitment, and give the group the assistance of your higher-level perspective.

The Follow-up Session

A final solution or recommendation will not always be hammered out at the end of a single session. In that event, schedule within a week an abbreviated follow-up session in which the original subgroups use the results of the first meeting as a starting point. If a consensus is not reached after this highly focused second session, the objections or the problems of the dissenters need very close scrutiny.

B. CONSENSUS: PRO AND CON

In Section 2A we presented our suggested meeting format for reaching consensus among a group of managers or professionals on issues such as the selection of organizational objectives, identification of organizational problems, establishment of priorities, or identification of alternative problem solutions. This format facilitates consensus among a large number of persons with maximum participation and time effectiveness. True consensus, however, is an elusive goal. Let's examine the group processes and interpersonal interactions through which consensus is achieved.

Win–Lose versus Win–Win Strategies

When, as children, you and I tossed pennies as a pastime, either you won and I lost, or I won and you lost on each toss. There was no way that the rules of the game would permit both of us to be winners. The strategy is one that has come to be known as *win–lose*. Of course, if we had continued the game long enough, we would have found that neither of us had won, but that, in fact, both of us had lost a lot of precious time. The win-lose strategy would have ultimately resulted in losses for both of us—it would have become a *lose–lose* strategy.

Many of us, as individuals or group members, go through life feeling and acting as though win-lose were the only workable strategy, with the too frequent result that in the long run nobody wins. If both parties to a conflict possess roughly equivalent power, an unproductive stalemate usually results. For example, a union or teachers' organization fighting management or the school board over salary matters has the power to shut down the plant or the school system by withholding services, while the management groups have various kinds of countervailing power — injunctions, automation, even the power to move the plant or go out of business. Superficially it may appear that one of the parties is the winner in situations like these. But a more thorough analysis would probably show that both parties lost ground with respect to where they both might have been and that they may also have created other losers who were not a party to the original struggle — students who suffered a reduced quality of education, local merchants who lost business, and so on.

If one party with power continually "wins" over others without power, the results may ultimately be catastrophic, as the history of mankind amply demonstrates. Sometimes, the win-lose strategy does create winners, but it also may create powerful losers who can make the cost of winning so great that it amounts to a loss.

There are situations in which win-lose is an entirely appropriate strategy. A poker pot is awarded to the player with the greatest skill at calculating probabilities, or at bluffing, or with a lucky position at the table, or a combination of all three. If the game is honest, losing in this case ultimately results for the most part in the losers either sharpening their skills or quitting the game for more profitable pursuits. Similarly, the salary increase pie is sliced in proportion to individual contributions, and the losers may be motivated to perform better as a result of losing. In the organizational world, however, where the future of a business and the fate of its members hinge on the quality and acceptance of decisions that involve concepts such as objectives, priorities, alternatives, plans, and change itself, the feeling of being a loser can be a major deterrent to progress. Hence the idea that if we develop a conflict resolution strategy that is *win-win* in nature, we stand a better chance of maximizing the effectiveness of our human resources. This is where the notion of *consensus* comes into play.

Consensus and Synergy

A group arrives at a decision in many ways. The decision may be imposed autocratically by the group leader[3]; it may be railroaded by a vocal minority; it may be made by a majority vote, or (in desperation) by the flip of a coin. It may also be reached by exhaustion, made by the last person to retain interest in the problem after all others have lost interest or departed the scene — physically or psychologically. All these are familiar decision-making methods. Some are entirely appropriate. Others reflect a need for stronger group leadership, or for the development of more productive interpersonal or intergroup relations. When the acceptability of the decision to the group is important, it is advisable to seek a consensus in preference to any of the other outcomes mentioned above.

We define consensus as a group decision that meets the following criteria: (The criteria themselves describe the process of reaching consensus.)

Each member can support the decision, even though he or she may not completely agree with it. This support is possible because each person knows that his or her viewpoint has been heard, understood, and given the consideration it warrants.

Each member exercises the responsibility to assure that conflicting ideas are afforded "air time," that listening and understanding are promoted, and that dissenters are drawn out and accepted by the group.

Each member looks continually for better solutions than any being proposed at the time (see Section 2C on brainstorming).

The importance of each person's role in achieving a truly consensual decision is obvious. Each acts as a monitor and a contributor. The tendency of consensual decisions is to be *synergistic* — that is, to be better than any of the originally held positions of the individual members. This tendency is the result of the ready acceptance of new ideas (the brainstorming effect), and of the consideration given to dissenters, whose rational or emotional objections spell trouble for any decision that would ignore them.

Consensus is not easy to achieve, but the advantages in improved quality and acceptance offset the costs in time and effort,

---

[3] A unique solution may also be imposed or dictated by the situation itself, but this is rare. Normally more than one alternate course can be pursued, and we are concerned here with the selection of the best one.

especially when the effects of the decision are widespread in the organization. The techniques and skills needed by individuals in the group are primarily those of active listening described in Vols. II and III.

Consensus versus Groupthink There are hidden hazards in the group processes involved in consensus seeking. The very cohesiveness that results from the active pursuit of understanding and sensitivity can lead to poor decisions. Psychologist Irving Janis uses the term "groupthink" to describe the syndrome in which the close group cohesiveness and the strong identification of each member with the group create illusions of unanimity, invulnerability, and morality.[4] These illusions may be so strong that they lead the group to bring pressure on any member who appears to question the direction the group is taking, the possible hazards involved, or the morality of the course of action. A strong degree of self-censorship may build up, quickly squelching any unpleasant or disruptive thoughts. Janis refers to this as "mind-guarding," a feeling on the part of the members that one of their duties is to protect their fellows from contamination by disruptive thoughts and feelings. Janis's book contains excellent examples, among them the Bay of Pigs invasion decision.

While this syndrome does not describe consensual decision making as we have defined it, the danger of groupthink is present whenever a strong group identity and pressure for unanimity coexist. As a group leader, you must take measures to guard against groupthink. These include warning your group of the danger, avoiding a strong directive stance as the formal leader, and deliberately withholding any statement of your own position so as not to foreclose other options on the group. You may also, as the leader, specifically assign to each member the duty of critically evaluating the group's progress.[5] An alternative is to invite an informed but disinterested

---

[4]Irving L. Janis, *Victims of Groupthink: A Psychological Study of Foreign Policy Decisions and Fiascoes* (Boston: Houghton-Mifflin, 1972).

[5]This may be counterproductive if there is a need for brainstorming during the session. As you will find out in Section 2C, critical evaluation is strictly forbidden during brainstorming. To avoid this potential obstacle, plan the decision-making process so that the brainstorming phase and the selection of final alternatives are carried out in two separate sessions scheduled at different times.

person to act as observer-evaluator to provide the group with a link to the outside world. The observer-evaluator should, of course, be thoroughly briefed on the reasons for his or her presence.

In spite of the dangers of groupthink, an effort to obtain consensus appears to be well worth the time and effort when (1) a number of people must freely contribute information and effort to the decision-making process, and (2) broad acceptance of the decision is required. While true consensus is an ideal that is seldom reached, decisions will be better as a result of the striving.

C. THE BRAIN-STORMING TECHNIQUE

At some point in your MBO implementation program, it may be instructive and useful for you to introduce your people to the *brainstorming* method of group ideation. Whenever two or more persons address themselves to a problem, it is important that each use his or her creative powers to suggest the best available course of action. The problem may be to evolve the best possible action plan in support of a key objective, to develop the most productive marketing strategy, or to hypothesize all the possible causes of a performance failure. Brainstorming provides a structured group environment designed to produce the maximum number of ideas in the time allowed, to get a high level of participation from every group member, and to tap the creative resources of the group to a degree that its proponents claim exceeds that of most unstructured group activities.[6] It is a process that requires little in the way of specialized

---

[6]There have been questions about the relative effectiveness of brainstorming and individual ideation. The following is an interesting test of the validity of the brainstorming rationale: Choose a warm-up problem. Divide the group as evenly as possible in numbers and skill level. Do not disclose the purpose, but take one subgroup to a separate room and ask them to list privately and individually all the solutions or ideas that they can produce in 10 minutes. Set a timer to sound an alarm at the end of 10 minutes, or assign someone as a timekeeper to stay with this group while you return to the others. With the second group, conduct a 10-minute brainstorm on the chosen problem. When both groups are finished, reassemble them and compile a complete list for each group, eliminating duplications. Cull out items that will not stand up to analysis, and compare the quantity and quality of the final lists. We will not venture to predict which mode will win out in your organization—it is difficult to equalize the skill and motivation levels between groups. In any event, even if brainstorming fails to win out in one of these simple generalized problems, you would be advised to try it on a real-life interdisciplinary problem with a group whose members each have a relevant skill but only a portion of the total range of expertise required.

leadership skills other than the ability to recognize and encourage those who want to contribute, and to exercise prompt and firm (but gentle) discipline on those who break the rules.

The rationale for brainstorming is that ideas latent in the mind of a group member are often prevented from being voiced because of the judgmental attitude that an unstructured group tends to have toward new ideas and suggestions. This attitude is usually very subtle, seldom appearing as ridicule or in other ill-mannered forms, but almost always as polite and rational analysis, which nevertheless has an unintended inhibiting effect. Someone who has an idea may fear rejection or being made to appear impractical in front of the boss or influential colleagues. There is also a natural hesitancy to make suggestions that are in another person's area of competence, out of respect for that person's position or expertise.

Brainstorming establishes a norm of acceptance rather than criticism, in which every idea, no matter how wild and impractical, is considered valuable as a springboard for modifications that might make it workable. Freedom from criticism by others also appears to reduce the tendency to be too critical of one's own ideas. This type of criticism occurs while the idea is still unspoken, and tends to *keep* it unspoken. Proponents of the brainstorming technique further contend that this tendency to censor oneself can prevent partially formed or subconscious ideas from emerging into consciousness where they can be verbalized and examined. The benefits of brainstorming, then, come from the release of ideas bottled up in the subconscious, the removal of inhibitions that prevent their expression, and the cross-fertilization effect as members of the group build on one another's ideas and suggestions.

The rules of brainstorming are simple:

1. *Try for the maximum number of ideas in the time available.* If possible, allow the session to proceed until the flow of ideas stops. Do not call a halt prematurely, however — a 30-second silence may simply mean that the ideas are still coming but are not yet ready to be verbalized. You may often be successful in restarting the flow by calling attention to an idea previously mentioned and suggesting that the group build on it. Maintaining a rapid tempo also minimizes the time available for judgmental analysis and helps to enforce rule 2.

2. *Allow no judgment, analysis, or critique.* There will be time for this later as the group culls from the list the ideas to be pursued further. The leader's most crucial task is to prevent any discussion of an idea,

except for a request that it be repeated or clarified (in the fewest words possible). Even *favorable* comments about an idea should be discouraged, because they tend to focus attention on that idea to the exclusion of others as yet unsubmitted. The leader should be very firm in enforcing this rule.

3. *Encourage members of the group to build on one another's ideas.* As we mentioned above, this helps to keep the ideas flowing, but its main purpose is to trigger the ideation process and to produce ideas that the same number of people working individually would not generate.

Before turning your group loose on an actual problem, try one of the warm-up exercises that follow. This will familiarize you with the technique, warm up the group to the ideation task, and help establish the norm of acceptance. During this warm-up, explain the rationale to the group. Attempt to develop the acceptance norm from the beginning by encouraging all members to participate fully. Tape the proceedings, or use at least two secretaries to record alternate ideas. Anything less will slow down the action and result in

Drawing by Stevenson;
© 1977 The New Yorker
Magazine, Inc.

"It's a task force of the best brains in the country, but so far it hasn't jelled."

fewer ideas. If you use secretaries instead of a tape recorder, provide them with flip chart stands and plenty of paper. Blackboards are usually inadequate. They fill up too fast and you will lose ideas when you have to erase.

It is important to preserve all ideas, because the next step is to eliminate those which do not warrant further consideration, and finally, to select the top few for implementation or detailed study. See Sections 2A and 2B for help in carrying out this final selection process.

WARM-UP EXERCISES IN BRAIN-STORMING

1. List any suggestions that might help solve the following problem:

   A four-story department store, after modernizing its elevators, was still plagued by complaints from women shoppers about the amount of time spent waiting for elevators. No floor space can be given up for more elevators or for escalators.[7]

2. List all the ideas you can think of for reducing shoplifting in a drug or department store.

3. List all the possible uses for discarded double-edged razor blades.

4. List ideas for the improvement of the quality of public education at the elementary or secondary levels.

5. List the "most wanted inventions" for inclusion in the first issue of a journal devoted to the stimulation of creativity.

D. ROLE TAKING AS A TEACHING TECHNIQUE

Success in implementing MBO depends heavily on how well the joint objective-setting and the performance-review processes are carried out. In most organizations, both these processes require some behavior change on the part of the managers and the subordinates involved—a change from the way they have been doing things. Learning theory indicates that one of the best educational tech-

---

[7]Adapted from W. H. Newman, C. E. Summer, and E. Kirby Warren, *The Process of Management: Concepts, Behavior and Practice* (Englewood Cliffs, N.J.: Prentice-Hall, 1972), p. 286.

niques for changing behavior is to provide practice in the desired behavior itself, rather than to tell people *how* to change or to work on their attitudes to promote change. It is often assumed that attitudes affect behavior. While this is undoubtedly true, there is increasing evidence that changing the behavior directly (or in this case practicing it) changes the person's attitude toward it. Thus, if joint goal setting is the desired behavior, and if both attitude and lack of skill are standing in the way, a method that involves practice can provide the needed skill and also help create a more receptive attitude toward the change.

Role taking[8] is one such method. This technique can take many forms, but we will confine our suggestions to a format that we have found particularly useful in training managers in the crucial one-to-one contact, in which a discussion with a single subordinate is held to set objectives or to appraise performance.

This format involves three individuals, who take the roles of manager, subordinate, and advisor-observer. All three are provided with common background information on the situation. In addition, the "manager" and the "subordinate" each receive a role sheet describing what his or her unique perception of the situation is to be and given certain facts not known to the others. For example, the "manager" may be instructed to push for the establishment of goals requiring technical skills while the "subordinate" is instructed to appear concerned because he or she has insufficient training in these same skills. The "boss" will typically be asked to show concern for broader issues than the "employee"; the latter will have narrower interests but more knowledge of day-to-day problems of which the boss is unaware.

This type of role taking, in which neither of the principal participants has full knowledge of the other's role, is called a *closed-role* situation. Role taking in which both participants have access to all the information is called *open* by contrast. A number of such situations appear in Vols. II and III. See the exercises at the end of this section for examples of closed situations.

The observer in the closed-role situation usually has access to

---

[8]Often referred to as *role playing*. We recommend that you internalize the role-*taking* concept because of the negative connotations of the word "playing," for example, "fun and games," "play acting," "phoniness," etc.

the roles of the two principals. This is necessary if he or she is to report to the principals on how effective each was in drawing out hidden facts and feelings from the other. On the other hand, if the observer is to be rotated into one of the principal roles (described later as one of the variants of the basic role-taking format), it is better to withhold the principals' role sheets and confine the observer's role simply to watching for and recording instances of various specific behaviors that are representative of productive or non-productive discussions. Examples are offers of help, active listening, acceptance of new ideas, nondirective questioning, etc. In either case — open or closed — the culmination of the observer's role is to feed back to the principals what he or she has observed.

The conditions created in role taking are likely to seem rather artificial and strained to the participants in their first introduction to the process. It is, in fact, a process with a substantial risk of failure the first time around. However, with proper preparation of the participants and a thorough understanding by you, the leader, of what you can do to minimize risk and maximize learning, role taking can be of great help when introducing MBO into your organization.

The risk element enters because the participants have imperfect information, different values, and individualized goal perspectives. A degree of conflict is thus introduced. These conditions are, of course, typical of real life and the advantage of undergoing this type of conflict in a simulation is that by exploring (with the help of the observer) the sources of the conflict, the participants can re-handle and practice the situation until the conflict is reduced. This opportunity is not often present in real-life situations. However, though the risks involved in the simulation are much smaller than in real life, they are still much *greater* to the participants than passively absorbing advice on how to conduct a performance appraisal or an objective-setting session. Role taking involves learning by *doing* and, as Engel[9] puts it in his excellent manual on the construction of role-taking exercises, it is necessary to "learn how to learn" in order to get the maximum benefit from role taking. Most adults are accustomed to a formal educational setting, in which listening and taking written exams are the only activities required of the learner. The experience of being thrust into a role-taking situation for the first

---

[9]H. M. Engel, *Handbook of Creative Learning Exercises* (Houston: Gulf Publishing, 1973), pp. 73-77.

time is somewhat analogous to the first session in the water for one learning how to swim. The suggestions that follow are designed to enhance the process of learning how to learn so that your experience with role taking can produce maximum benefits in minimum time.

Some Common Problems

It is only fair to forewarn you, as leader, of some of the symptoms indicating problems that often arise in role taking. You may encounter such initial reactions — either before or after the first role-taking experience — as these: "I'm just not an actor," "This situation is too unrealistic or oversimplified," "I don't know enough about the situation to have a good idea of how to handle it," or "This situation was foreign to me . . . I would have reacted differently in my own surroundings." Comments of this kind are quite frequent and reflect the "newness" and lack of understanding of what the learning situation requires of the learner.

There are a number of things you can do to facilitate this understanding. First, your group should be made to understand that acting is neither required nor desirable. In fact, one of the most unproductive behaviors you will find in role taking is the tendency of some participants to "ham it up." The only acting called for is acting *naturally* — in a way which does not violate the integrity of one's personality, but which is directed toward the resolution of the problem situation, using as guides the principles of MBO that have been covered in self- or group study.[10]

Persons who just do not seem willing or able to inject themselves into the situation require some assistance. It is desirable to go over the preliminary briefing (which we recommend you provide to all participants — see the procedure below) in greater length with those who report these feelings after a warm-up role-taking session.

Some persons immediately see the possibilities in the techniques of role taking, but object that they do not have enough

---

[10]A frivolous or "ham-acting" participant is quite likely to report triumphantly, "I fired the so-and-so." You will require patience at such a point. A matter-of-fact comment on your part to the effect that "This wasn't the purpose. Let's go back now and see if you can salvage him," or "That's more a confession of failure than anything. I suggest you switch roles and see how *he* would handle the situation," can help provide such a person with a stronger sense of purpose.

information, or that the situation is foreign to their experience. The latter is particularly prevalent when an industrial situation is presented to participants in a government agency, hospital, or other nonprofit organization. While the situations included in this manual involve activities with which managers or managerial aspirants in any organization should be familiar, you should feel free to make changes in position titles or other background information that you think will be helpful for your group.

The problem of not enough information is best confronted in your introductory remarks to the participants. Two attributes of successful managers are (1) the ability to adapt to new situations, and (2) the ability to ask the right questions to gain information in a fuzzy situation so that a sound decision can be made. The situations provided here are deliberately stingy with information to provide this type of challenge to managers, as well as to introduce the necessary level of conflict. Furthermore, it is quite realistic to present a manager with a situation in this form, since it is typical in real life that the first indication a manager receives of a problem is rather vague. Likewise, it is unusual for the agenda of a meeting to specify in detail all the results that may be achieved or the assignments for further work that are likely to be required. These are points that you should make forcefully to your group to overcome the "realism" obstacle.

Another frequently encountered problem in role taking is poor observer performance. There are two major causes. The more important is the difficult and somewhat ambiguous role of the observer. The observer is not really part of the action, but must provide sensitive feedback to both participants following their session. The observer must be able to recognize and understand the positions of both participants, and to perceive the strengths and weaknesses of their respective behaviors. This is facilitated if the observer has access to both roles, so that he or she can provide feedback, for example, on points of difference which should have been resolved but were not. This means that the observer role can be more demanding than that of either of the other participants. The best way to overcome problems arising from the difficult observer role is to emphasize the importance of good performance to the success of the whole process. You should also provide extra preparation for the observers, as we describe in the variants to the basic process later in this section.

The other cause of poor observer performance is that the observer feels "lower on the totem pole" than one or both of the participants, and is hesitant to provide feedback. This may appear to argue against the random selection of the groups-of-three on the spot, and for determination of the groups in advance. You must make this decision based on your knowledge of your organization. We can only say that the chances for full implementation of MBO are lessened if managers are unwilling to accept (and subordinates unwilling to give) feedback of the type required for productive role taking.

Still another, but probably less important, problem exists if your training session includes nonsupervisory persons and they are assigned the role of the boss. Since you will be working with managers and perhaps some high-level staff specialists with managerial potential and exposure to various leadership styles, this is not likely to be a major problem. If it occurs, assignment of the nonsupervisory person as an observer (with the attendant problems mentioned above) is one alternative. We prefer that such a person be encouraged to take the managerial role and be given extra preparation for it. We do not, however, recommend that the *first* assignment of non-supervisors should be taking the role of boss with their real-life boss.[11]

Improvisation: How Much?

A question that often arises is how much the participants should be allowed or encouraged to improvise questions and answers if the facts are not spelled out in the background information or on the role sheets. We encourage improvisation, for two reasons. First, the discussions may become sterile if the participants cannot depart from the printed facts. Second, improvisation is *realistic.* It is rare that you go into a meeting with your boss or a subordinate with all answers to all possible questions prepared in advance. In the role-taking situation, the "boss" should be encouraged to ask any questions related

---

[11]However, such a role reversal can be very valuable in the more experienced organization, or in one that has undergone a team-building experience. While this is outside the scope of this manual, we recommend the *1974 Annual Handbook for Group Facilitators* (La Jolla, Calif.: University Associates), pp. 227–237, as a source of further information.

to the discussion issues that a boss would normally ask a sub-ordinate — to test the depth and quality of his or her thinking, the degree to which he or she has considered alternatives, and so forth. The "boss" should not ask questions that would not normally be answerable by an employee, but should ask about things that an alert, well-informed employee would be expected to know about the job.

The person assigned to the subordinate role should anticipate questions that might arise, just as he or she would do in real life, and have in mind the kinds of answers (including "I don't know, but I'll find out!") that would be appropriate in an actual situation — as long as the answer does not violate the facts or conditions stated in the role, and can stand the test of further questioning by the boss.[12]

The results of such improvisations should be considered as "new facts," which are then used in generating or revising goals and objectives, appraising performance, etc.

There is a subtle difference between improvisation and fabrication, however. You should encourage your group to refresh their memories on the productive interviewing techniques covered in Vol. II, Unit 8 and Vol. III, Unit 7. This will help ensure against "dead end" questions that can be answered with a "yes" or a "no" or with a fabricated explanation of *past* events that must be taken at face value. The more productive line of questioning, of course, inquires into the "how" and the "what," with emphasis on future action. For example, "What can we do to make up lost time on Project X?" or "How can I help you to get the job done more effectively?"

A Basic Procedure for a Role-Taking Session

We have selected the following basic procedure as one that will satisfy the needs of most organizations. You may modify it along the lines of one or more of the variations described. This procedure offers all members of your group the maximum opportunity to practice the desired behavior, and is easily adaptable to any of the

---

[12]It may occasionally happen that the duo comes to agreement on goals or plans that are wildly optimistic or frivolous. This indicates a failure on the part of the "boss" to require credible performance. Observers and leaders must be sensitive to this failure of one or both participants to become really involved in the role. (See footnote 10 for suggestions.)

variations. However, unless the group size is limited to approximately twenty-one people (making seven teams, each consisting of a boss, subordinate, and one observer), you may find that the demands on a single trainer/leader are excessive. It is obviously impossible for you to monitor seven discussions on anything but a sampling basis. Even the routine problems and questions arising from seven or more discussions will tax fully your ability to provide guidance and feedback to teams who need it.

If your group does not consist of a multiple of three, you may designate the one or two most capable persons as roving observers to assist you or to sit in with teams who do not appear to be making progress — or you may wish to recruit a member of your training component to fill in as a role taker.

The steps of our basic procedure are (1) the introduction, (2) preparation of the participants, (3) the role-taking session, (4) observer feedback, (5) group discussion, and (6) the recycle. Allow 2 to $2\frac{1}{2}$ hours to complete the process, including a single recycle.

1. **The introduction**

   This is your opportunity to explain what role taking is all about, to state the objectives of the session, to legitimize the process as a serious undertaking, and to answer questions. Allow 15 to 20 minutes total. The briefing you have had in reading the preceding section of this manual should provide you with the necessary ammunition. If you don't feel comfortable about this, we suggest that you practice your presentation with a colleague who has read the foregoing material. Then jointly critique your efforts. It is very important that you approach your group with confidence and a sense of mission. Your positive attitude will help to establish a productive climate. Your introduction should include:

   a. The objectives of role taking

   b. A description of what is going to happen

   c. The importance of the observer role

   d. Cautions against acting

   e. Encouragement of improvisation

   f. References to the interviewing techniques covered in Vol. II, Unit 8 and Vol. III, Unit 7

   g. A question-and-answer period

2. **Preparation of the Participants**

   a. Announce the makeup of the teams, or select them at random by counting off (by sevens if you want seven teams).

   b. Pass out the sets of background information and role descriptions to each team, assigning the roles at your own discretion or allowing the team members to volunteer for the roles.

   c. Allow 5 to 10 minutes for the group to read and absorb the information and familiarize themselves with their roles. Caution them against discussing their individual descriptions with each other, but encourage discussion of the background information to assure common understanding of the general situation.

   d. Call for questions on the background information from the groups. After answering these, offer to answer privately any questions on any of the three roles. If there are more than two or three individuals in each role who have questions, it is best to take all the bosses aside and quietly answer their questions, out of earshot of the others; then do the same for all subordinates, etc. While you are involved in these discussions, encourage the rest of the group to make notes and formulate questions and positions in preparation for step 3.

3. **The Role-Taking Session**

   a. Begin the session by arranging the teams so that boss and subordinate are face-to-face, with the observer positioned to observe both.

   b. Start the action and allow the discussion to proceed for about 25 to 30 minutes. A reminder at the halfway point will help to prevent teams from getting bogged down on one issue. Give a 2-minute warning at the end to allow the participants to bring the discussion to an orderly close, and to alert the observer to make final notes for the feedback session. Be alert for participants who continually consult their role sheets before speaking, or who make such comments as "but it says on *my* sheet . . . ." This indicates poor understanding of the process or insufficient time for preparation. In a case like this, it is best to stop the action, allow more time to prepare, and assure understanding before proceeding further.

4. **Observer Feedback**

   Allow 10 to 15 minutes for the observer to give his or her impressions and comments to each role taker, and to give them an assessment of the success of the action. This should be a three-way conversation, with the principals asking for clarification where needed and commenting on their own and the other's performance. As the leader, you will obviously not be able to monitor all the conversations, but do not be concerned. Most participants report that this session of feedback from their peers is the portion of the process that provides the most insights.

5. **Group Discussion**

Reassemble the group and ask for comments from observers on problems they saw arising during the role-taking session, or for significant insights that they or the participants obtained. The participants should also be encouraged to reveal their insights. It is often productive to ask the group how their session compared with the last appraisal or work-planning session in which they participated with their boss or a subordinate.

Allow this discussion to continue for 20 to 30 minutes, or for as long as the sharing of experiences and insights continues. This step of the process and the preceding observer feedback session provide the basis for the final step for this session.

6. **The Recycle**

This new level of learning and awareness should be applied immediately, by repeating the simulated discussion using role-reversal, rotation, or one of the other techniques described in the variations below. The recycle should start with step 3 without further introduction other than a recap of the results of the group discussion.

Variations of the Basic Format

1. The introduction and preparation steps may be done at the end of a day's training session to allow ample time for the participants and observers to review the pertinent materials in Vols. II and III, and to become thoroughly familiar with the situation and their roles. The remaining steps are then carried out at the following session. This procedure also allows time for you to meet in a group with all those taking the same role (particularly important in the case of the observers) to ensure that each person understands the potential significance of all the facts and feelings described. (This extra step may be especially helpful in the group's first exposure to the role-taking process, but should prove less necessary as your group becomes more experienced.)

2. As part of the preparation step, you may ask your group to practice one of the open role-taking situations (all facts known to both participants) provided in Vols. II and III. If they have done a thorough job of self-study before your session, they will have already gone through these exercises with a colleague. If not, this variation will elevate

everyone to a minimal skill level, in addition to providing a warm-up for the more complex situations included in this manual.

3.   A demonstration role session may be useful at the introduction or preparation step (or as a recycle event, as described below). This involves one pair carrying out their roles in front of the remainder of the group who, with your help, collectively act as observers. You may ask for volunteers to take on this task, or may assign two persons experienced in joint goal setting or other interviewing skills to demonstrate the desired behavior.

This particular variation may be carried further, with several sets of volunteers successively going through the same exercise, and their performances compared. This measures and takes advantage of the learning that takes place by observation rather than by doing. Although you are certain to notice a steady improvement in performance from pair to pair in this variation, the learning process is more efficient for most people if they learn these skills by doing. This is why we recommend the total group participative mode that is our basic format. This variation is also very time-consuming and, frankly, boring to continue until *all* have had a chance to demonstrate.

Video- or audiotaping each session is an excellent way of comparing selected portions of successive demonstrations for quality. To do this without wasting time retrieving the taped footage you want to play back, station yourself at the recorder during the demonstrations, making notes of the digital counter readings whenever a significant example, good or bad, is taking place.

4.   A number of variations can be introduced into the role-taking or recycle steps:

a. *Role-reversal or rotation*— You may ask the boss and subordinate— or all three persons— to change roles and repeat the exercise. This is applicable mostly to an open-role situation in which there is no private information. The realism of the closed-role situation is reduced with the reversal, since at that point all information is known to both principals. Nevertheless, some additional learning results from the comparison of one's own performance with that of the predecessor in the role.

b. *The participant observer*— You may specify a more active role for the observer by instructing him or her to take the part of a consultant and offer advice during the session to the two principals. Such a role requires somewhat more sophistication and experience in role taking on the part of the observer, and is best introduced at later stages in the learning process. Although frequent interjections by the "consultant" interrupt the action and may make it more difficult for inexperienced participants to get into their roles, this is not a completely unrealistic type of intervention. A number of organizations employ an outside consultant to sit in with a manager and subordinate in the initial stages of MBO implementation.

c. *The alter ego*— Another way of using the extra persons in the group, as an alternative to supplemental observers, is to assign each one as an alter ego to a boss or subordinate. This person silently takes the same role as his partner, thinking through his responses and noting differences between his and those of the active member. These notes can be fed back to the active member at the end. Alter egos can also change places with each other — that is, the silent member becomes the active participant, and vice versa — and carry out a repeat session, leaving the third person in his or her original role. It will be instructive to observe the changes that take place in the third person's responses with the change of partners. The observer should be especially alert for changes not only in the content but in the mood of the discussion as the alter egos change places. You can build in these changes by selecting alter egos with known differences in interpersonal style in a demonstration setting as described in 3 above.

5. Following the group discussion step, you may substitute a demonstration session as the closing event of your meeting, instead of going on with another role-taking (recycle) situation. This demonstration may be carried out by a team that has done particularly well (or poorly) in step 3. You may have made this determination yourself when circulating among the teams during their sessions, or you may base your decision on the comments of the observers or principals during the group discussion.

Your experience and ingenuity may suggest other variations, or may even lead you to adopt a basic format different from the one we have presented here. But regardless of the format you choose, a major prerequisite is a full explanation to the participants of the purpose and the personal benefits they may receive. Assure yourself of their willingness to give it a serious try. If your best efforts meet with resistance from a few, it is best to give them the option of sitting it out, at least in the beginning. Impress upon those who do participate that a role is something more than a sheet of paper, and you will be well on the way to success.

41

E. ROLE-TAKING EXERCISES

The background information and role descriptions contained in the following exercises will satisfy the needs of most organizations in initiating an MBO program. They may be adapted for use in various types of organizations by simple revisions such as job title changes, or by more complex ones such as the introduction of a technical task rather than the more general conflict situations contained in the exercises. The names of the participants have been chosen so that both men and women can feel comfortable with the assigned roles. An alternative that provides more realism is to have the participants use their real names in the discussions.

The situations use the closed-role technique and are relatively complex. Simpler situations of the open-role type, which you may wish to use as warm-up exercises, are included in Vols. II and III of this series.[13] Don't be concerned if your people have already worked with these on their own. Practicing with a new partner often produces quite different results and enhances the learning process.

---

[13] You will find these in Vol. II, Exercise 8, and in Vol. III, Exercises 7, 8B, and 9.

EXERCISE 2A

OBJECTIVE SETTING
IN THE TRIANGLE CHEMICAL RESEARCH AND
DEVELOPMENT DIVISION

**Instructions for
the Leader**

The Triangle Chemical situation offers the person taking the boss role the challenge of communicating the existence of a crisis in the organization to a highly competent but single-minded "subordinate," as they go through their first joint objective-setting session. It also tests the "subordinate's" adaptiveness and creativity, as new information is presented that challenges old and cherished ideas.

You can enrich this exercise by providing the participants with blank forms patterned after Fig. 6 in Vol. II. This will ensure that their technical and business problems will be discussed in a framework that forces consideration of and practice in the use of key results areas, standards, and other concepts involved in the MBO flow process.

We recommend role-reversal or rotation in this exercise, so that all three participants have the experience of being the "boss" in conducting this critical session — the first formal contact between "boss" and "subordinate" in the MBO implementation phase. Although the first use of the exercise may have greater impact because of the secrecy factor, subsequent uses in which all participants share the secrets are still useful for practicing interviewing skills and building on the performance of the first team.

THE TRIANGLE CHEMICAL RESEARCH DIVISION

General Background on Triangle Chemical Company

(Information possessed by all participants)

Triangle is an innovative, highly profitable organization, producing space age materials for industry and, more recently, for the consumer. It was formed about 20 years ago by a small group of chemists, metallurgists, and materials scientists, who started the business on a part-time basis while teaching at the University, and who later left the teaching field to make Triangle their full-time career. The rising tide of space technology rapidly lifted the company to the $50 million sales level, as the demand for exotic materials exploded. The founders were canny enough to put a great deal of the research and development effort into adapting their products for consumer and industrial applications. Thus, as the space boom subsided, the firm managed to maintain a steady, although slower, year-to-year growth trend in both sales and earnings. As a measure of Triangle's emphasis on research and development and its success in converting to a civilian market, the company can claim today that 50 percent of its sales are in product lines that did not exist 5 years ago. Today's products consist of a wide variety of "wonder glues," sealing and caulking compounds, and high-strength plastics for households and appliance manufacturers, in addition to the super-light alloys, heat shields, and low-temperature materials still being manufactured for the aerospace industry.

Although Triangle is strong both technically and financially, the newly elected president, a Wharton School of Finance graduate who was hired from outside the company 5 years ago, has established new corporate objectives which emphasize consolidation and cost improvement, but still call for continued growth. There is concern that several basic patents are reaching or have recently reached expiration, and although a number of improvement patents obtained through the years have kept Triangle in the forefront technically, several new competitors — foreign and domestic — are marketing products that are very similar to some of Triangle's older offerings, at slightly lower prices.

The new president has embraced the concept of MBO, and recently hired a consultant to conduct a series of familiarization seminars for all managers and for key technical and professional employees.

The situation involves Sandy MacBride, director of plastics research and development, and a product design engineer, Lou Hunter, in the plastics R & D section. Both have completed the seminars and are preparing to meet for the joint establishment of the objectives to which Lou will give top priority in the first MBO review period. MacBride has just completed a similar session with the vice president of company R & D.

Objective Setting in the Triangle R & D Division

(Information possessed by the boss, Sandy MacBride)

You are Sandy MacBride, manager of the plastics R & D section of Triangle; your group of top-caliber chemists and engineers have been largely responsible for the growth in this portion of the company's product lines in the last 8 years (5 of which were under your management and 3 under that of your predecessor).

You have recently gone through the first joint objective-setting session with your boss, the vice president of R & D, and for the first time in a long while you feel that the pressure is on and that your section is under the gun. In spite of your section's record of innovation, there has been a noticeable flattening of the profit curve. You and your people have, of course, been aware of this, but in your session with the VP you were surprised at the amount of evidence that the VP had picked up from various sources, which indicates that things are worse than they appeared, and that they may get a lot worse before they get better. Much of this evidence was obtained by your VP from the marketing and manufacturing VPs. You confirmed its accuracy by talking directly with several marketing and production people, though at first you were skeptical that things could have gotten this bad without your knowing about it. You attribute your ignorance of the situation to your associates' hesitancy to upset your creative efforts by burdening your people with day-to-day problems. Whatever the reason, it is apparent that:

1. *Manufacturability of some older products is less than optimum.* An analysis of manufacturing problems, which you requested from production, indicates that your people may have been passing their new products along to the plant a little too rapidly in their eagerness to take on new challenges. Excessive manufacturing costs and quality problems are evident in some of the older products, especially now that they have come under pricing pressure from competitors. While higher markups on new products helped mask this basic problem for some time, recent inability to compete in the marketplace has brought it into the open.

2. *Marketing problems are also multiplying.* You regard it as an especially ominous sign that your friends in marketing, who have always been delighted with your creative and prompt response to customer needs, have recently been suggesting that perhaps fewer new products and a bit more attention to maintenance of the line might be appropriate.

They cite product variability from shipment to shipment, failure of products to perform properly in certain new customer applications, and other incidents that have shaken the confidence of the sales force in the plastics product line.

Lou Hunter, a product development engineer in your section, is the first to be scheduled for an objective-setting session with you. Lou is a highly creative young engineer whom you inherited with your group when you took over 5 years ago. Previous experience in manufacturing operations has given Lou a good knowledge of the business, and you believe he has management potential — he is decisive, analytical, and highly motivated. However, Lou has had an unusual number of problems in his relationships with the production people during the procedures that Triangle follows in transferring newly developed products from R & D to manufacturing responsibility. You therefore have some reservations about Lou in the human relations area. Still an engineer at heart, Lou apparently does not realize the importance of interpersonal relations in carrying out a management job.

As you understand it, objective setting under MBO rules involves some degree of negotiation between boss and subordinate. You have analyzed your operation and have resolved to try to get each person in your section to allocate 20 percent of his or her time to cost improvement projects in the forthcoming review period. As a fall-back position, maybe you can get each person to select his or her three worst "problem products," study them for cost reductions and quality improvement, and take appropriate action. In any event, you intend to convince Lou Hunter to commit some real effort to tackling several such projects if the 20 percent target doesn't seem appropriate as your discussion develops. The work that Lou will have to do with the production people will be valuable experience and will, at the same time, give you a better reading on Lou's management potential.

You are not looking forward to Lou's predictable reaction to "joint" objective setting, but there is no use delaying — let's get it over with!

Objective Setting in the Triangle R & D Division

(Information possessed by Product Engineer Lou Hunter)

You are Lou Hunter, product engineer in the plastics R & D section, under the leadership of Sandy MacBride. Sandy is a good manager, as far as you are concerned, leaving you pretty much on your own and giving you every opportunity to pursue your own ideas—as long as the product fills a market need. Your relationship is a two-way street, however. You have contributed more than your share of major product developments, and you feel that Sandy's respect for your work is no more than deserved. A number of Triangle's largest selling products are your "babies," although you don't have much interest in following their progress after they leave your hands. After all, your talents are best used to develop new products, not to manufacture or sell established ones. As a matter of fact, you wish that those who *are* responsible for your products in the plant would do what they are getting paid for. The production people are continually fouling things up, taking shortcuts, using poorly maintained equipment, and ignoring the niceties of the processes that you have so painstakingly developed.

If there is one aspect of your job which you dislike, it's the unpleasantness of dealing with the production engineers during the product transfer procedure. They are apparently determined right from the start to compromise the quality of the product by insisting on relaxing many of the safeguards you have built in, claiming that you can't run a production plant like a development laboratory, and complaining about "unreasonable specifications," and so on.

At one time, you had thought you would make a career of production engineering, because of the excitement and the feeling of being on the front line. But you quickly perceived that there was more boredom than excitement; and so much depended on trying to get lazy, incompetent, unmotivated people to do things right—an extremely frustrating, seemingly hopeless task.

Sometimes you feel that working with people just isn't your thing. You get a real thrill out of solving a difficult product design problem by yourself. It's so much more satisfying to know that you personally did the job, even though there may also be satisfaction in getting things done in cooperation with others. You are not particularly looking forward to the MBO system. The sessions with the boss are sure to mean more interference in your activities. You sense that

Sandy, too, feels a little uncomfortable about your forthcoming objective-setting session.

You have reviewed the status of your current and pending projects, and have decided that you can make the greatest contribution by concentrating all your attention on transferring your top-priority projects to production and then starting on an exciting new idea you have for an auto tire surfacing compound. The compound will provide tremendously increased traction on snow and ice, potentially obsoleting snow tires, studs, and chains. Meanwhile, you will make as much progress as possible on the two other products you have under development. You expect that this will not meet with much resistance from Sandy, who has always been solidly behind you on all your ideas. Besides, what you have scheduled is an extremely demanding load, probably greater than that of any other engineer in the section. This session shouldn't take more than a few minutes, and then you can get back to work!

Objective Setting in the Triangle R & D Division

(Instructions for the observer, who also has the information possessed by Sandy MacBride and Lou Hunter)

You are to observe the objective-setting session between Sandy and Lou, feed your impressions back to them, and later to the assembled group if instructed to do so by your session leader. You are to be alert for and to note any examples of productive (or nonproductive) interaction between the two principals, and to rate the discussion qualitatively for its success in generating objectives that will be helpful both to the individual and to the organization. [Since you have read both roles, you are aware of the informational and perceptual gaps that exist between the two persons. You should also assess the effectiveness of each party in bringing out and resolving any conflict or erroneous assumptions either one may have going into the session.][14]

The following list of questions will help you carry out your important feedback role:

How well were the interests of the organization served? The interests of the individual? Was there an agreement that considered one at the expense of the other? If so, were commitments made to resolve the situation in the future?

Who dominated the conversation? Did the boss "tell" or "sell"? What kinds of learning occurred? About each other? About the company and the competitive environment? About themselves?

In your opinion, were the objectives that were reached sound? Clear, specific, measurable, achievable, important? Did they represent a change or merely a documentation of what was already being done?

Were the objectives backed up by a sound action plan? Were checkpoints established for review?

To what degree were the employee's long-range interests and career considered?

Did the employee ask for, or did the boss offer, help? What kind?

[How skillful was each in eliciting the feelings of the other, and the important background information that the other possessed?

Did any information that was important to the objective-setting process remain unused at the end of the discussion? Would its introduction have changed the result?]

---

[14]Note to the leader: Bracketed material should be omitted if you do not intend your observers to fulfill this function.

50

SECTION 2

EXERCISE 2B **A PROGRESS REVIEW
IN THE CRYSTAL CITY PUBLIC WORKS DEPARTMENT**

Instructions for the Leader The Crystal City situation is very rich in potential conflict and in opportunities to practice and examine productive interviewing and problem solving in the progress review session. Do not hesitate to recycle this exercise several times with the same group. There is enough content so that inexperienced groups can continue learning through several cycles.

The situation can easily be modified to fit an industrial setting. If industrial terminology will help gain acceptance and involvement, we suggest the following changes:

Government	**Industry**
From: Conservative council	To: Former management "milking the business"
Public works tasks	Maintenance and facilities tasks
City manager/director of public works	Plant manager/Plant engineering manager
Water plant expansion	Plant-effluent treatment facility

The realism of the progress review may be enhanced by providing the objectives on a completed form of the type shown in Fig. 3 on p. 86 of Vol. III, and by supplying the teams with blank forms to use in modifying objectives for the next period. As an alternative, you may work directly on the figure following the general background on Crystal City.

THE CRYSTAL CITY PUBLIC WORKS DEPARTMENT

General Background on Crystal City

(Information possessed by all participants)

Crystal City is a small but rapidly growing community of 12,000 people, which was fortunate enough about 12 years ago to be the closest residential community to a newly relocated major plant of Gigantic Enterprises, manufacturers of electric and electronic equipment. The firm has grown and attracted a number of smaller supplier firms to the area. It has in turn contributed to the rapid growth of the local liberal arts college, where enrollment has increased from 1200 to nearly 5000 during the 12 years, leading to new construction and a heavy increase in traffic.

Since Crystal City is the closest residential community to the Gigantic plant and has educational facilities, adequate shopping areas, and other services, it has attracted most of the plant's supervisory, management, professional, and technical people. This has led to a demand for additional services, and also for better quality services.

For a number of years, a very conservative city council maintained as their top priority the holding down of the tax rate, until problems began to multiply beyond the capacity of the city administration to cope with them. Traffic has approached the intolerable point, paving is deteriorating faster than it can be repaired, drainage improvements are needed to prevent flooding of a major new residential development (the flooding commenced with the construction of a new interstate highway bypass), water mains are no longer able to provide the pressure required for fire fighting during peak usage periods, the sewage disposal plant needs enlarging, and so on. A major expansion of the water plant is under way, scheduled for startup on July 1 of this year.

Citizen pressure for change in the past election brought about a sweeping change in the makeup of the council, and a substantial tax increase has been enacted to give the administration some ammunition to fight with. However, after all these years, the administration is playing a fast game of "catch up" and, as must be obvious, the public works department is feeling the pressure.

A new director of public works, Lee Jones, was appointed about a year ago, replacing the person who had been in that position (or its earlier equivalent, the street and water superintendent) for 22 years. The council is anxious to see some real improvement in the affected areas, and the approved budget has allocated to Lee a larger pool of resources with which to operate, including a number of new positions in the public works department.

Three months ago, the city put into effect a new system called "management by objectives," which resulted in a performance appraisal procedure in which progress against mutually agreed-upon objectives is the basis of the appraisal. A quarterly progress review, followed by an annual overall appraisal on the anniversary date of the installation of MBO, has been planned.

Three months ago, Lee sat down with Chris Henry, the city manager, and set up some primary objectives for the coming year. It is now time for the first scheduled (3-month) review of Lee's progress. A copy of Lee's objective statement is attached. It does not include technical activities, since these seem to be going well, but concentrates on two areas, staffing and coordination with other departments.

The other departments under Chris Henry are personnel, public safety (including police and fire), planning, finance, parks and recreation, and social services. There is also an assistant city manager and the city attorney.

PUBLIC WORKS OBJECTIVES FOR YEAR 19__

PREPARED BY:
EMPLOYEE: L.P. Jones, Director-Public Works
MANAGER: C.F. Henry, City Manager
PREPARED ON: January 2, 19__

Key Results Area	Objective	Progress Review Comments Date: March 27, 19__
Staffing	a) Fill newly authorized positions within next year as follows: 3 supervisors, by 3/1/__ 1 engineer, by 2/1/__ 6 water technicians, by 7/1/__ b) All new hires to be high-quality people (as determined by performance ratings) c) Stay within recruiting budget of $750 for travel expenses, ads, etc., for the year.	
Coordination	a) Organize task force with public Safety, Planning, and Finance, and present recommendation to council by 4/15 on needed changes at major intersections and rerouting of traffic. b) With assistant city manager, start quarterly public works newsletter for citizens to keep them well informed of future programs and progress. First issue to be distributed with water bills by 4/1.	

First Quarter Progress Review of Lee Jones, Director of Public Works

(Information possessed by C.F. Henry, City Manager)

The date is 3/27, 19__.

You are about to conduct a quarterly progress review (first quarter) with Lee Jones, the public works director. You are generally satisfied that Lee is handling the job as a competent professional. All major projects are reported by Lee to be on schedule. However, you are concerned about progress in staffing. While Lee apparently accepts the new EEO requirements on minorities and "special groups," you wonder if Lee really is giving this matter the time and attention the council expects. Also, you wonder if the recruitment of the water technicians should be completed sooner than planned to allow some training before the plant expansion is completed; you think you may press for this.

According to your records, only two of the ten new positions have been filled, the engineer and one supervisor; both are white males. Likewise, there is apparently no reply on Vietnam veterans, in spite of your memo of February 16 to all department heads requesting that priority consideration be given to this large group of unemployed whenever feasible.

The coordination tasks, you feel, are just not getting off the ground. You intend to explore this further. Lee is not noted for teamwork, and you have as one of your own major commitments to council the welding together of an effective team. You deliberately made Lee the chairman of the traffic task force to provide "practice."

As of this moment, however, you have the uneasy feeling that some "quick and dirty" proposal on the traffic situation is going to have to be presented to the council on April 15. You would rather get the item rescheduled for the May agenda than present some poorly thought-out recommendation. You recognize the difficulty of the problem. However, on the newsletter, there should be no excuse for not getting the first issue out on schedule. Improving Public Relations is also one of your major promises to the council.

You know that Lee feels that some of these things are just added burdens, but you are convinced that he should delegate more to subordinates. You plan to advise on the need for doing this, and to try to find out why the director hangs on to so much of the work. You also intend to raise some questions about the suggestion program. You have been getting some complaints from Personnel that Public Works is not using this excellent tool for getting employees' ideas; you feel the director should make an all-out effort on this.

There is a knock on the door and Lee enters.

First Quarter Progress Review
of Lee Jones, Director of Public Works

(Information possessed by Lee Jones)

The date is 3/27, 19__.

   You are about to discuss the first 3 months progress toward meeting your targets with your superior, Chris Henry, the city manager of Crystal City. You have reviewed your goals for the year and have made some notes for yourself:

1.   You feel you and most of your department have really put out in the last 3 months just to cope with the day-to-day problems.

2.   On recruiting new people, you are having a difficult time meeting everybody's requirements. There just aren't that many qualified minority persons and women around, and Personnel has changed signals on you just last week and asked that you give preference to Vietnam veterans. If you had known this, you might have done better, but anyhow, how do you tell which group has top priority, veterans or who? Personnel vaguely referred to a memo on this, but you haven't seen anything in writing. Who has time to even read the mail these days? Anyhow, you've hired two good men, an engineer and a supervisor, both whites. That's a start.

   On the water technicians, at least, you've got some breathing space. The latest meeting with the contractors indicated that the expansion may be about 3 months behind schedule. (You'll have to mention this to the boss. You're embarrassed and a bit apprehensive about this because you sort of misled Chris — no fault of yours — by reporting to him only a couple of weeks ago that everything was on schedule.) You note from the latest expense report that you have already spent $500 on recruiting.

3.   All this stuff from personnel is beginning to bug you. On top of the Vietnam veteran thing, they're poking into your business and complaining that you're not using the suggestion system! You've never yet seen a suggestion system that really works — delays on getting approval by the manager on awards (and the small size of the awards) make this more irritating than satisfying to the employees involved.

4.   Coordination! You wish you hadn't agreed to do this task force thing. You really don't know why the boss appointed you as chairman in the first place. It should have gone to the planning director — neither he nor the public safety director seems anxious to get things moving,

and you've only got about 3 weeks to get your recommendation ready. You're about ready to give up on this one. How can you do all you're doing and still find time to lead a group on a complicated task like this?

This newsletter is another thorn in your side. If it's performance they want, let your work speak for itself! Why blow your horn in a newsletter? Besides, you spend so much time answering citizens' pet peeves and complaints in person and on the phone, that there's little hope of getting anything written. If only you could trust your subordinates enough to give them some of your work, things would be better. But their mistakes are *your* headaches and the boss is holding *you* responsible.

5. In retrospect, you thought MBO meant joint objective setting, but in looking back on your first session, it really seems to you that you didn't have much to say about it, especially in the coordination tasks.

6. Wow! What a day this is going to be! You even resent the time this appraisal discussion is going to take. You're doing your best. Isn't that enough? Well—let's face it! The boss is waiting for you.

Crystal City Public Works Department

*(Instructions for the observer, who also has the information
possessed by Chris Henry and Lee Jones)*

You are to observe the quarterly progress review between the boss
and the subordinate and feed your impressions back to them and
later to the assembled group if instructed to do so by your session
leader. You are to be alert for and to note any examples of productive
(or nonproductive) interaction between the two, and generally to
rate the discussion for its predicted effectiveness in achieving the
desired results. [Since you have read both roles, you are aware of
the informational and perceptual gaps that exist between the two
persons. You should also assess the effectiveness of each party in
bringing out and resolving any conflict or erroneous assumptions
either one may have going into the session.][15] The following list of
questions will help you to carry out your very important role:

Were there differences in perception as to the employee's progress?
Regarding the importance of the objectives? The reasons for their
importance? Regarding the priorities among objectives? Were these
differences resolved?

If differences were resolved, how was this done? Dictatorially?
Persuasively? Was it necessary for anyone to back down?

Were any creative solutions found to the problems of performance?
What was the source of the ideas?

Was help sought by the employee? Volunteered by the boss? Did the
boss show commitment to really providing the help needed?

Was there adequate focus on improvement of results, overall?

Were new or revised objectives established for the next review period?

[How effectively did the discussion bring out and resolve the
following points?

The concern of the boss over Lee's ability to work with others, and
Lee's failure to understand the reason for the coordination task

---

[15]Note to the leader: Bracketed items should be omitted if you do not intend your observers
to fulfill this function.

The fact that the memo written by Chris on hiring of Vietnam veterans was not read by Lee

The resentment Lee has toward personnel over the suggestion system, and the boss's vulnerability in passing along hearsay on the subject

The surprise that Lee had in store for the boss about the waterworks startup delay

The parties' different views on the importance (and the problems) of delegation

Lee's feeling (perhaps unjustified) that there was some pressure used by Chris in gaining acceptance of the objectives

Lee's problems meeting the April council meeting deadline, and the boss's recognition of the situation and resulting wish to postpone the presentation]

OTHER ROLE-TAKING EXERCISES

1. The open-role situations presented in Exercise 8 of Vol. II, and in Exercise 7, 8B, and 9 of Vol. III, are suitable for use in a group role-taking session as described earlier in this manual. Any of these exercises can be used for demonstration or as a warm-up.

2. The following open-role situations may also be helpful in testing a group's understanding of (a) the MBO process as a whole, or (b) the joint objective-setting process.

   a. You have just completed, with selected subordinates and higher-level managers, a seminar describing the purposes and general operating methods of an MBO system. You and one of your key subordinates are both concerned over the seemingly large additional burden that MBO places on both managers and subordinates, and are wondering what MBO will do to help both the organization and you as individuals. You are about to discuss this together over coffee. You would both like to "believe" and hope that the discussion will provide some reassurance. (Note to leader: A review of the introductory unit of Vols. I, II, or III will be helpful before the group takes this on.)

   b. You and your boss have set a date a week from today for a meeting at which you and he will set some objectives for you for the coming 3-month period. The idea of joint objective setting is rather new and strange. You consider yourself a "good soldier" and rather enjoy the challenges often thrown at to you by the boss to tackle a particularly difficult job. You appreciate the boss's confidence that you will take on the tough ones without question and without a lot of supervision and help — and you are quite willing to trust the boss's judgment as to what is important and what you should be working on. On the other hand, you (as the senior person in your unit) and the boss both see a need for more help for some of the newer employees (and for one or two whose performance is marginal). Knowing your "good soldier" attitude, the boss has asked you into his office to explain why you should hold your meeting next week as planned, and to seek your advice on how to proceed in meetings with the marginal and newer employees in the unit.

SECTION 3

IMPLEMENTING YOUR ORGANIZATION'S MBO PROGRAM

A. GETTING STARTED— DEFINING AND ATTACKING THE BARRIERS TO MBO

The exercises we have presented in this manual can help your organization develop understanding and skill in several areas that are crucial to the success of a new MBO system: assessing the need for such a system in the first place, reaching consensus on corporate objectives, strengths, or key results areas, and conducting the important manager-subordinate interactions that are the foundation of the system.

However, we haven't yet addressed the question of how to introduce this material in your organization so as to ensure maximum impact and effectiveness. We wish there were a formula that would answer questions such as whom to involve as trainees, when and in what order they should receive the training, and so forth. In lieu of such a formula, we will offer some suggestions based on experience, which we hope will be translatable into your organization.

First, we are convinced that the key personnel in any organization can simultaneously acquire, by individual study and self-analysis, the knowledge and insight required for productive group discussions and decision making on the future of MBO in the firm. But it is not likely that everyone will do the required study unless it is known to be a major concern of managers at the highest level of the organization, and unless all are convinced of the benefits MBO can bring. Furthermore, even top-level managers may need to be convinced before they will expect their subordinates to do individual study.

Top-Level Involvement: Key to Successful Implementation

We, therefore, first recommend that the executive staff (the top person and his or her direct reports) take on the responsibility of evaluating MBO: reading the texts, sampling the exercises, and assessing the potential of MBO in a meeting designed around both the exercises at the end of Section 1 and the three discussion questions below. These questions explore the barriers that stand in the way of organizational change.[1]

MBO is almost certain to call for some kind of organizational change, in organization structure, job classification, compensation criteria, managerial style, employee attitudes, planning skills, or openness of communication. An analysis of the barriers standing in the way of change is a prerequisite to change itself. The following three questions will help you develop the information you need to make a sound decision on whether to proceed further with an MBO system:

1. What specific changes will an effective MBO system require of our organization?
2. What barriers or restraining forces stand in the way of these changes?
3. What measures are available for eliminating these barriers?

---

[1] If you are in middle management or in charge of a component in which you intend to implement MBO on your own, the approach we describe is still appropriate. However, you should assure yourself that you have the support of your immediate supervisor, and that both of you recognize the difficulties that such an approach entails. Specifically, you must recognize the danger that your goals may diverge from those of the overall organization, and the problems involved in interlocking your objectives with other components whose managers may not share your views.

The force-field problem-solving model described in Unit 10 of Vol. II will help identify the barriers and determine the best ways to overcome them.

Unit 6 of Vol. II will be especially useful as a preparation for this top-level meeting. You should also read the text of Section 1 of this manual. The top manager may choose to lead the meeting, or may elect to participate as an equal with the other members of the group to practice the principle of power equalization described in Unit 8 of Vol. II. If the manager does not act as leader, a high-level training and development person from your organization may do so, or else you may decide to bring in an outside facilitator.

Training at Lower Levels of the Organization Assuming that top-level management decides to proceed with a formal MBO program for the whole organization, the design of further group training will depend on the readiness of the key individuals who will be involved. This judgment must be made by the managers based on knowledge of the attitudes and level of understanding of their immediate subordinates. If the collective judgment is that the key people need practice in joint objective-setting or performance review, large groups (up to thirty), mixed as to function and managerial level, are appropriate. If, on the other hand, the purpose of the training is to stimulate thinking about functional or component objectives, or functional key results areas (see Vol. II, Unit 4), groups limited to the functional or component manager and his or her immediate subordinates will in most cases produce optimum results. It may be appropriate to expand the group to include three organizational layers — for example, the marketing manager, the managers reporting to him or her, and all the supervisors reporting to them. However, too wide a range of rank, for example, the chief executive officer and the first-line foreman, in a group can inhibit free discussion. Your knowledge of your own organization will determine the best grouping. In any case, we recommend that thirty people be the upper limit when discussion and interaction are important to the quality and acceptance of the decisions reached.

Once the top-level team has determined that MBO *is* needed, there is no reason to hold lower-level meetings for the same purpose. However, it is useful to assign lower-level teams to the task of defining more precisely the *areas* of need, and their priorities. It should be thoroughly understood by all that the decision has been made to proceed, if that is indeed the case.

A more democratic approach is to hold such lower-level meetings before the top-level decision is made. You must make it clear, however, that the decision to implement organization-wide MBO is the responsibility of top management, and that the purpose of lower-level meetings is to develop necessary information for top-level decision makers, not to delegate the decision itself. This should not raise any real problems with the "populists" in your organization. If the executive office decides to adopt organization-wide MBO, there will be ample opportunity at all levels for participation in decision making as implementation proceeds.

To summarize — training sessions following the decision to implement MBO are of two general types:

1. *Skill-building sessions,* in which mixed groups of substantial size (up to 30) can practice one-to-one interaction, using role-taking methods, and develop understanding of the principles of MBO, through discussion in small subgroups as described in Section 2A of this manual.

2. *Component meetings,* composed of the manager of the component and his or her subordinates, designed to resolve issues such as overall component objectives, key results areas, and other basic guidelines for participation in the MBO program.

Participation in these meetings should be extended to the lowest level at which objectives are to be set and progress is to be measured — generally the level of the individual professional or technical employee.

We believe that the ultimate success of the MBO system depends on the one-to-one relationships between managers and their individual employees, which makes the skill-building sessions especially important. There is a tendency to overlook this type of training and to concentrate on the component meetings. Don't neglect skill-building when faced with the understandable pressure to get objectives set and put the MBO system into operation.

Integrating MBO with Your Budgeting Process

Where does the budgeting process fit into an MBO system, or vice versa? Does the budget dictate what objectives are possible, or do objectives dictate what the budget should be? Should the MBO implementation program be tied to the ongoing cycle of budgeting?

The first question is a "chicken or egg" dilemma, answered by the fact that we have to start with *something.* If we assume that MBO enters our thinking at a random point in time, the "something" is necessarily an approved level of funding, upon which we super-impose the MBO process. Figure 3 illustrates the ultimate effect MBO has on the budgeting process. Initially, the budget has primacy (point A) over MBO and MBO must conform with "reality." Eventually, the two become inextricably related, as shown. From this diagram, we can conclude that the timing of the initial MBO implementation need not await the approval of a new budget. The initial impact of MBO on the budget comes via the comparison of budget allocations with (1) the goals and priorities determined in the MBO process (point B), and (2) the improvement potential in the departments. Both comparisons become the basis for the next budget revision, but the MBO implementation need not mesh closely in time with the budgeting process. In fact, it is advantageous to begin MBO at a time in the fiscal year that can be expected to be less hectic than the budget period.

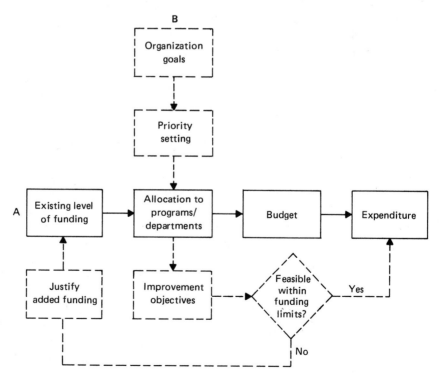

FIGURE 3
The relationship between MBO and the budget.

B. SELECTED FEATURES OF SUCCESSFUL MBO PROGRAMS

A successful MBO program requires a great deal of tailoring to fit the unique characteristics of an organization. The following hints, tips, and suggestions (submitted by practitioners who have built successful MBO systems) will help you cope with some of the more common questions and problems that are likely to arise in your own implementation program. For example, questions such as: How far down in the organization should I try to use MBO? How often should we review performance? How can we keep paperwork to a minimum? How do we keep employees and managers interested in the system? The list of ideas that follows is designed to stimulate the search for answers to questions such as these. Challenge your people to prevent or overcome implementation problems by developing their own list of rules, reminders, and remedies—or practice brainstorming with them and build upon these.

Take every opportunity for adjacent levels of management (top and middle, middle and first-line) to explore *together* the progress, problems, and successes of the MBO system, and suggest ideas for improvement. If lower levels are left out, they may regard MBO as just another campaign from headquarters and not give it their full attention.

Emphasize improvement needs and brainstorm regularly for ways to improve the MBO system itself. The system should not be blindly accepted in its initial form. A static system cannot effectively administer a changing organization.

Eventually carry MBO to the lowest level at which discretion can be exercised on the job, and/or direct supervision is not present. Some organizations (see Vol. II, Unit 7) carry it, through a program of job enrichment, to the lowest worker level, eliminating the supervisor and relying (successfully!) on self-control on the part of the worker.

Redo Exercise 1B, "Diagnosing Organizational Needs," periodically to measure change in the maturity of the organization. Don't attempt to answer the questions privately—handle them instead in discussions among interdisciplinary or interlevel teams.

Reach a consensus if possible, but if not, probe the reasons for disagreement. Unfortunately, such discussions do not work in an organization where there is little competence in interpersonal relations, or where team identification is nonexistent. Training is available in these areas.[2]

Consider establishing an "objective manager"[3] for each major objective requiring interdepartmental action and extensive lateral communication. Similarly, assign the monitoring responsibility for the overall MBO program to an authoritative person reporting to top management.

Before you come down too hard on people who say, "It's impossible to plan on meeting objectives in my job," don't overlook the unplanned, unpredictable demands that are typical of some jobs. If that is the nature of the work, and if readiness to respond is important, you should require only a minimum number of objectives from the incumbent, and concentrate on objectives that will improve the effectiveness of response.

Analyze the *reasons why* you have too much to do to spend time thinking about MBO, or other changes in your organization (e.g., recurring crises, uncontrollable priority changes from outside, lack of managerial guidance, fuzziness of mission, meetings, etc.). Set objectives for handling these problems first. See the time effectiveness exercises in Unit 3 of Vol. I.

Schedule performance progress reviews with employees well in advance, with backup dates in case of emergency. Do not wait to set an alternate date until the emergency occurs, or you may never set one.

Adapt the frequency of your progress reviews to the nature of the job or project involved. Excessively frequent reviews lead to a "soap opera" syndrome — the feeling that you could skip six episodes without missing a thing.

Destroy all performance appraisal forms that use multiple-choice questions instead of commentary or, at the very least, require specific supporting comments.

If you hold high-level home office reviews of certain important objectives, invite key individual contributors to attend and participate when-

---

[2]See the *Annual Handbooks for Group Facilitators* (La Jolla, Calif.: University Associates, Inc.), published each year starting in 1972.

[3]The idea of the objective manager, originated by the U.S. Public Health Service, is described by Dale D. McConkey in his excellent book, *MBO for Non-Profit Organizations* (New York: AMACOM, 1975), Chap. 11.

ever feasible. If travel expense limits attendance, the area manager may decide to skip a meeting and delegate a subordinate to attend instead (explaining to top management why this is being done). The manager assumes the risk that his or her interests may be poorly represented, but this risk can be minimized by proper selection of the subordinate and improved communication and trust between subordinate and manager.

If your organization is scattered, schedule some top-level reviews in the field. Exposure to subordinate managers and specialists by top management (and vice versa) help build cohesiveness and trust.

Face your marginal-employee problems squarely. MBO requires competent employees and managers. Set action plans and objectives for training, coaching, and other forms of development. A forceful statement of your feelings is often appropriate and helpful if other attempts fail. As a final measure, consult your policies for appropriate disciplinary action, including removal.

Assign to staff people the objectives of upgrading staff services, improving line-staff relations, and making new technology available to the organization.

Use the continuing narrative summary technique[4] for written progress reports; avoid generating a new piece of paper at each reporting period. Whenever an update is required, the manager can return his or her copy to the employee.

Top management must resist the desire to see every progress report. Limit most reports to the two people involved — manager and subordinate. Failure to do this is the major cause of the paper mill.

Schedule some time at each session for review of priorities, i.e., "Do we or do we not continue to report on — or work on — the project, and how often should we report?" A decision here is a must, to prevent the session from degenerating into meaningless reporting from force of habit.

Attempt to divide review session time into 25 percent for review and 75 percent for revision and forward planning. (Exception — the annual performance appraisal; see Vol. III, Unit 6)

---

[4]This summary is a narrative report format in which each month's or quarter's progress is typed as a continuation of what went before. Thus, the report provides a history of the project from the beginning to the present. Typically, each addition is limited to a paragraph or two. Only two copies are prepared, one for the immediate manager and one for the employee.

If an effective joint problem-solving review procedure is now in effect for major objectives, projects, or programs, don't scrap it and start over. Do not develop a parallel system, either — MBO should not duplicate what you are already doing well. If your present procedure is not productive, devote some time in each review to analyzing *process.* For example, "How productive are our review meetings? Is there a better way to conduct them?"

Make MBO fit your existing routines and systems from the start. Minimize disruptions and revolution. Make it evolutionary. See, for example, Fig. 3, for relating MBO to the budgetary process.

Your highly competent performers will regard MBO as so much "Mickey Mouse" at first. They know they are *already* doing a first-class job. Enlist their aid in helping others (see the final role-taking exercise in Section 2), and don't burden them with objective-setting forms that merely force them to document what they are already doing. Contract with them orally. However, don't assume that all who resist are competent. Incompetents also resist, for other reasons. *Know* your people!

C. ALTERNATIVE MBO SYSTEMS

In this series, we have described a generalized system of MBO which we believe is adaptable to any organization. In so doing, we have used a terminology and format with which we feel comfortable, but which may seem overloaded with jargon, forms, and other trappings alien to your organization. This needn't indicate that MBO is not for you. The system can be as variable in practice as your unique situation demands.

The cases described below are real-life examples of two different approaches to implementing MBO. The two systems in-involved vary widely in terminology used, degree of formality, and detailed procedures. Case A concerns the management education division in the adult and continuing education school of a major university. Case B describes the system developed for a small social service agency at the state government level.

As the leader of a group, you may find these cases useful as bases for critique by your people or as catalysts for suggestions on implementing MBO in your own operation.

CASE A

One Manager's Recommendation on an MBO System
for His Division of a Major University

MEMORANDUM

January 2, 19____

TO: A. T. Starbuck, Dean
FROM: W. P. Walsh, Director
SUBJECT: Suggested performance evaluation procedure,
           management education division (MED)

In response to your request for my recommendations on a modified format for individual work planning and review for specific use in MED (or elsewhere if it should prove to meet the needs in other areas), I would like to bring you up to date on the measurement and appraisal system we have in mind. Also included are some editorial comments based on past participation in similar systems.

This proposal is in part an adaptation of some of the features of the division's existing plans of work. It is based on two pieces of individualized documentation, the first of which we call Performance Guidelines and second a Work Plan and Review Chart.

A description of the purpose and content of each follows. (The attached exhibits contain hypothetical examples of items that might appear in an individual's guidelines and plans. At this point, they are meant for illustration and clarification only. The detailed drafting and finalization of performance guidelines and work plans would be undertaken as a joint effort by the individual program planners and the director.)

Performance Guidelines (See Exhibit I)

Part A A detailed listing of the major activities, duties, and responsibilities (including responsibilities for coordination and relationships with others) of a specific position. The list may vary somewhat depending on the individual holding the position (for example, to utilize his or her major strengths) and should be reviewed and modified within appropriate constraints with and by each new incumbent. Briefly, part A is a detailed statement of *what* is to be done.

Part B A broad statement for each of the activities in part A to indicate the degree of accountability expected. It would focus on questions of *how well, how much,* etc.

Note: Some writers may prefer to combine parts A and B into a single statement. For example, an A and a B statement might read:

> "A2. Develop noncredit programs and other educational activities to meet the assessed needs of the public." (The duty—i.e., *what*)
>
> "B2. The quality and quantity of program development efforts." (The measure of accountability—i.e., *how well, how much,* etc.)

while a combination statement might read:

> "Responsible for developing noncredit programs, as measured by the quality and quantity of such development activity."

Part C Quantitative and/or specific indices to be used to determine how the goals listed in part B are being achieved through the individual's work. For example, referring to the A2 and B2 statements above, the C2 entry might read:

a. number of new programs developed/planned
b. specific examples of unique programs not offered elsewhere
c. specific innovations in educational process and technology
d. specific instances of client group reaction
e. program evaluation reports
f. etc.

Note that the C items need not be quantitative, and in particular that each single index, whether quantitative or qualitative, should be used by the director in conjunction with all the other indices to arrive at an overall judgmental rating of the B item involved. This helps to avoid relying too much on the "numbers game," and requires that we focus on what we are really interested in (in this case, the quality and quantity of programs developed through the individual's efforts). Note further that one single "reading" of performance may not mean nearly as much as an assessment of the *trend* of performance over a series of reviews. The C items are intended to set a uniform standard for assessing a trend over a period of time. This is similar to the way a uniform EKG procedure gives a physician the basis for determining deterioration or improvement over a series of measurements, when each individual measurement might be deemed "within normal limits."

Work Plan and Review Chart (See Exhibit II) The purpose of this document is to take into account (1) that a given review period might not encompass all the activities listed in part A of Exhibit 1, (2) that there will be times when priority activities will command essentially all an individual's discretionary effort during a review period, and (3) that the pressures of ongoing routine (non-discretionary) activities may make it difficult to remain focused on the creative, or nonroutine tasks that an individual sets out to do.

The work plan and review procedure forces some advance thinking about what the priority projects are for the forthcoming measurement period and what specific tasks are to be completed (or milestones reached). The procedure provides a continual self-measurement of progress, *if* it is used and not put on the shelf. It is also helpful in the periodic exchange of ideas between the director and the specialist as to what each must do to eliminate obstacles, redefine or clarify goals, solve problems, etc. Exhibit II is broken down into the following areas:

Duty/Responsibility— This is a reference to the activities listed under A in Exhibit I.

Goal— This is a brief statement of the *specific* achievement desired for the time period being planned. For example, "Prepare and staff, phase II of the Supervisory Development Institute," or "Reach a go/no-go decision on a televised (ETV) management science program at Northern Community College." The overall goals may be outside the time frame being considered (normally 3 to 12 months), but at least one milestone should be within that time frame.

Milestones— These are statements of who needs to do what by when and with whom in order to achieve or show progress toward the ultimate goal. For example:

Explore feasibility with Community College by 3/1
Plan program content by 5/1
Recruit lecturers by 6/1

Tape first six sessions by 7/1
Air first telecast 7/15

Time Allocation— This is optional, but obviously some estimate of the number of trips, days of travel, concentrated planning time, meetings, etc., needs to be a part of any rational plan, to avoid overextending personal resources. Some managers and participating specialists may prefer to leave this space (or even an extra foldout sheet) for notes and comments on the review sessions.

The work planning and review process is not commonly thought of as a performance appraisal per se, but rather as a progress-reporting-problem-solving activity. The performance appraisal is more properly a summation of the judgments of the achievement of the B-item goals in the performance guidelines document. The work-planning process does, however, contribute to appraisal of performance by helping rank and weigh the importance of the B-item goals, and provides indices of achievement over and above the C items listed in the guidelines. It also serves the purpose of helping all participants to keep critical target areas in focus at all times. If properly used, this process can result in improvement of the performance itself, as well as in the appraisal of the results.

Of course, the whole procedure is likely to be viewed as just so much extra work by both manager and employee. If, in fact, the benefits do not exceed the costs in terms of (1) a more fruitful and orderly planning process, (2) the early detection of incipient failure, and (3) a better understanding of the overall mission by all levels of the organization, then the procedure obviously should not be continued. Past successes have been noted when the goals are not rammed down the individual's throat, but are genuinely participative, and when lack of progress is viewed as a problem to be solved in a spirit of mutual helpfulness rather than a reason for criticism. In the absence of these emphases, failures have resulted, with the system degenerating into game-playing on both sides—and, of course, the ultimate kiss of death comes when a component merely goes through the motions, prepares "the book," and then puts it on the shelf.

EXHIBIT I

Performance Guidelines

FOR: John Rooney

POSITION: Management Specialist/Program Coordinator —
Industrial Sector

A. Activities

1. Assesses the needs of client groups for credit and noncredit educational activities through appropriate surveys, personal contacts, conference attendance, literature review, and other appropriate techniques

2. Develops noncredit programs and other activities to meet the assessed needs of the assigned sector of the public

3. Utilizes all appropriate resources and technology in the development of programs, such as the latest instructional techniques, appropriate college faculty, and outside consultants, to meet the specific needs of adult audiences

4. Exercises leadership in providing service to the entire region (in proportion to the needs), utilizing or coordinating with consortia participants where feasible, and within consortium guidelines

5. Participates in long-range MED planning by suggesting to the director objective and goal modifications, etc.

6. Represents the MED and the University to the public, and increases public awareness of the services offered and rendered, through personal contacts, publications, etc.

7. Etc.

B. Measures of Accountability

1. Accuracy and thoroughness of his assessment of the market and the need for his services

2. Quality and quantity of program development efforts

3. Etc.

C. Achievement Indices (shown for Measure of Accountability B2 only)

a. Number of new programs developed/planned

b. Specific examples of unique programs not offered elsewhere

c. Specific innovations in educational process and technology

d. Specific instances of client group reaction

    e. Program evaluation reports

    f. Etc.

Note: A wide variety of formats may be used to fit individual preferences. For example, A1, B1, and C1 might appear contiguously. (I happen to prefer a cover sheet grouping all the A items together; this allows me to review the list quickly from time to time to see what I may be neglecting in my planning, etc.)

EXHIBIT II

Work Plan and Review Chart

Work Plans for Calendar 19____

NAME: John Rooney

Duty/ Responsibility	Goal (What)	Milestones (When, What, with Whom, etc.)	Time Allocation
A3	Assess drawing power of recognized authorities from off-campus in increasing enrollment in capital budgeting workshop.	Select area of skill by 1/15. Contact major figures in field by 2/1. Select key speakers by 3/1. Plan and execute program (3d quarter). Assess economic and promotional success by 10/1.	Total 3 man-weeks (peaking in 3d quarter).
A1	Determine need for a special development institute for textile plant management.	Compile mailing list by 1/15. Determine sample by 1/22. Design questionnaire by 2/15. Analyze returns by 6/1. Recommend course of action by 7/1.	Total 1 man-week.
Etc.	Etc.	Etc.	

CASE B

How MBO Was Developed for a Very Small Organization

Developed by Michael W. W. Crump*, for a small group of social service professionals (3) and a secretary, all of whom were involved in close, interrelated work. The structure was quite flat with everyone reporting to one of the professionals (Director).

I. Strategic Planning Process

All work in this phase was done by the group as a whole. Rather than develop a mission statement, this group sought to narrow its entire job to a manageable size by answering four questions.

A. *What do we do here?* The group sought to make explicit its contributions to (1) the parent organization, (2) its clients, (3) the community at large, and (4) the group members themselves.

B. *What else should we be doing?* The group considered general trends in the services that the group provided, changes in the local environment, and their frustrations over opportunities they had had to forego because of lack of resources. This analysis caused them to focus on one new area of endeavor, and to assign it a rather high priority early in the planning process.

C. *How do we know when we have accomplished our major responsibilities well?*

1. (type of information required) Here the group analyzed the nebulous nature of the feedback they used to answer this question. Several suggestions for keeping records, and developing new sources of feedback were made explicit. This information was used later as a basis for control of the various objectives and their supporting plans.

2. (standards of performance) The discussions dealt explicitly with the levels of performance that were expected by the parent organization, needed to establish an appropriate presence in several areas served by the group, and required to provide each individual with the impetus needed to develop his or her own professional abilities.

---

*Syracuse University School of Management.

II. Objective-Setting Process

The group formulated specific objectives. These objectives were designed to be:

A. *Measurable.* Expressed in terms of (1) time, (2) cost (man/time units), (3) quantity, and (4) quality (making explicit the boundaries of a satisfactory result in ways other than time, cost, and quantity).

B. *Prioritized.* Once the objectives were established, they were rank-ordered in three groups of priority to aid in making subsequent decisions on resource allocation.

C. *Assigned as responsibilities.* Even though the work of the group members was interrelated, they sought to pinpoint accountability, create "job wholeness," and clarify mutual expectations by assigning responsibility for specific objectives to individuals. In the case of an objective that was assignable at this stage, the individual responsible developed his or her own plan for its achievement. In the case of an objective that was not assignable, the group as a whole began to plan the details for its achievement.

III. Specific Action Planning

Because some objectives had to be accomplished by the group as a whole, these objectives were jointly planned in detail. The planning met the following criteria:

A. Specific sequential milestones were identified.

B. Responsibilities for reaching milestones were assigned to individuals.

C. Individuals put plans into writing in the form of objectives for themselves.

D. The major components of the plans as assigned were written by the assigned individuals in measurable terms.

IV. Validation

Because this was the group's first experience in extensive planning, members went through the process of estimating the cost (time) of the objectives established. The total effort of each member was estimated and summed for each objective. The group found that it had committed about 38 percent of the total number of man-months available to it. The remaining 62 percent was allocated to keeping the shop open, and to other activities that could not be planned. The group effort in validation was a valuable learning tool for individuals in measuring their own commitments. Incidentally, validation is an important step in effective time management. (Steps I to IV were accomplished in a 3-day planning session.)

V. Mutual Agreement

Following the planning/objective-setting sessions, the director met with individual group members to reach a congruent set of expectations. At this point, the director established control and review procedures to provide for adequate feedback to all parties.

VI. Control

Control was defined as determining how plans are progressing in time to make changes if progress was not satisfactory. In the joint goal-setting process, the director analyzed each individual's plans with the purpose of setting up control points that would allow the director to determine if the plans were progressing satisfactorily. The initial responsibility for identifying these points lay with the individual. It was also the individual's responsibility to determine information needed to assess progress and to establish contacts with others inside or outside the group who might possess the information.

The primary means of control was a periodic review session between the director and the individual. The frequency of such sessions was established according to the following criteria:

A. *The requirements of the job.* Jobs in which substantial resources were being expended, which would have important results, or which were in a rapidly changing environment may require close supervision.

B. *The requirements of the individual.* Besides having different levels of skill, experience, and judgment, individuals have varying needs for structure and direction. (If the manager's role is to achieve by helping subordinates achieve, then individual needs are a perfectly legitimate factor in determining frequency of review.)

C. A formalized review for the purpose of feedback to the individual and for recording management information on individual performance was to be held at least quarterly.

The dates of review sessions were established well in advance and assigned a high priority. Postponements and cancellations were avoided if at all possible.

DEVELOPING YOUR OWN ALTERNATIVE SYSTEM: FORM VERSUS SUBSTANCE

A final word on the form your MBO system should take: it should fit the culture of your organization. The forms, terminology, procedures — strategic planning, objective setting, performance review — and the reward system should build upon whatever you find useful in your present system. *Be selective in your use of the material in these books — and at all costs avoid creating the impression that you are engaging in change for the sake of change itself.*

Above all, as you explore the literature of MBO for further ideas, don't let jargon (including ours) stand in your way. If the terminology seems foreign, stilted, or otherwise at odds with your needs, translate it into your own language as the authors of these two alternative systems — Case A and Case B — did. In the final analysis, it is your concern with *substance* rather than form, with *improvement* and the way you apply these general principles to your own situation, that will determine the outcome for you.

INDEX

Page numbers in *italic* indicate charts or graphs.